W

whip

expert cakes • meringues • ice creams • soufflés • batters • sauces

maggie mayhew

LAUREL GLEN

San Diego, California

Published in the United States by
Laurel Glen Publishing
An imprint of the Advantage Publishers Group
5880 Oberlin Drive, San Diego, CA 92121-4794
www.advantagebooksonline.com

Copyright © MQ Publications Limited 2001
Text © Maggie Mayhew 2001
Project Editor: Nicola Birtwisle
Text Editor: Coralie Dorman
Designer: Elizabeth Ayer
Photography: Janine Hosegood
Stylist: Vanessa Kellas

Kitchen equipment kindly supplied by
Gill Wing Cookshop, London, England

All notations of errors or omissions should be addressed to Laurel Glen Publishing,
editorial department, at the above address. All other correspondence (author inquiries,
permissions and rights) concerning the content of this book should be addressed to MQ
Publications, 12 The Ivories, 6–8 Northampton Street, London, England N1 2HY.

Mayhew, Maggie.
Whip: the expert guide to whipping techniques / Maggie Mayhew.
p.cm.
Includes Index.
ISBN 1-57145-587-6
1. Cookery. I Title.
TX651. M35 2001
641.5'89--dc21
Library of Congress Cataloging-in-Publication Data available on request.

1 2 3 4 04 03 02 01

Printed and bound in England by Butler & Tanner Ltd

NOTE
Recipes using raw eggs should be avoided by infants, the elderly,
pregnant women, and anyone with a compromised immune system.

contents

introduction

Whipping isn't just for cream and meringues. There are lots of things you can do with this magical technique. To whip, or whisk, means to incorporate air into a mixture to give a frothy or stiffened consistency. Cakes and soufflés just wouldn't exist without air, as they depend on it to help them rise and to improve their texture.

When making sauces, on the other hand, the whisk and the whipping process are useful for different reasons. In roux sauces the technique lets you cook the sauce over a higher heat, making it less likely to form lumps. Rapid whisking also helps reduce the risk of the sauce burning on the bottom of the pan. When making mayonnaise-style sauces, the whisk combines fat- and water-based ingredients to make an emulsion with a stable, creamy consistency.

The most basic piece of whipping equipment is, unsurprisingly, the whisk. They're available in many shapes and sizes, from simple balloon whisks to hand-held electric models. In some cases a fork can be used to achieve the same result but this will require a much faster wrist action.

The best way to whip by hand is to hold the whisk loosely between the thumb and forefinger, like a pencil, allowing the handle to rest on the side of the hand. Then whip with a circular action from the wrist, as lightly and quickly as you can, to allow pockets of air to become trapped within the mixture.

the basics: whipping cream

It's important to start with chilled cream—either heavy or light cream—and use a cold bowl, preferably ceramic, stainless steel, or glass. The best style of whisk to use is a balloon whisk, a hand-held electric mixer, or an old-fashioned hand-held rotary whisk. Whip quickly to begin with until the cream starts to thicken and attains the consistency of custard. Now's the time to reduce the whipping speed so you don't overwhip. If you continue whipping for a short while, the cream will begin to hold its shape but will drop easily from a spoon. At this stage it is of spooning consistency. It will have some texture but won't hold its shape for long.

If you whip for a few seconds more, the cream should start to hold its shape and will have a glossy sheen. Once you get to this stage, the cream is perfect for serving, as it will thicken slightly on standing or piping.

Make sure you don't overwhip your cream. If you keep whipping past this stage, the cream will form stiff peaks and become too thick and buttery in texture. If overwhipped cream is left at room temperature it may even separate out into curds and whey.

the basics: whisking egg whites

Whisking is a vital process in the making of a meringue. When egg whites are whisked, they increase their volume and become frothy, light, and airy. They will achieve a better volume if they are left at room temperature for a couple of hours, and not used cold, straight from the refrigerator.

Use a balloon or egg whisk for the best volume and texture, but if you are not used to whisking by hand, or speed is of the essence, an electric hand-held or tabletop mixer will be fine. Separate the eggs, allowing the whites to drop into a grease-free, nonreactive bowl. If any egg yolk falls in with it, remove before starting to whisk. The easiest way to do this is to use one of the broken shells—for some quirky reason the yolk is attracted to the shell. Whisk quickly and lightly in an even, steady movement. The egg whites will become frothy but still liquid.

If you continue whisking past this stage the whites will become stiff but smooth. This is the stiff peak stage, when sugar or syrup can be added. A good way to check if this stage has been reached is to tilt the bowl. If the egg whites begin to slide out of the bowl they need further whisking.

If sugar is to be added, lightly sprinkle it over the top, a spoonful at a time, whisking well in between each addition. When the egg whites are very stiff and glossy the remaining sugar or ingredients can be folded in gently with a metal spoon to prevent knocking out the air.

Now that you've learned the basics, it's time to start whipping! Shown on the next four pages are all the pieces of equipment you'll ever need.

equipment

twirl whisk This manual whisk is very flexible and useful for working around the entire base of the bowl or pan. Great for preventing lumps in sauces.

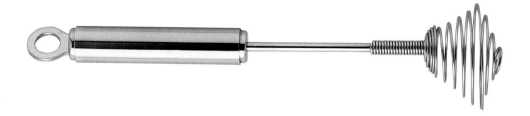

eggbeater The all-time reliable kitchen favorite, this whisk is a snap to use.

spiral whisk Ideal for whisking sauces in shallow dishes and for getting into the corners and bends of a bowl.

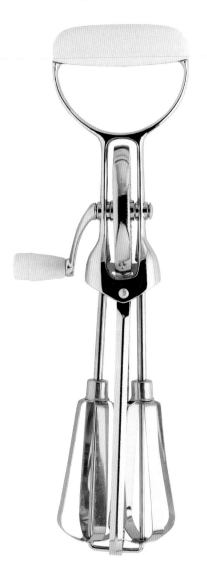

egg whisk More wires than an ordinary balloon whisk make this good for aerating egg-based sauces and egg whites for meringue.

sauce and dressing whisk This small whisk is perfect for making tiny quantities. Very light and easy to use in smaller containers.

balloon whisk The classic whisk, this can be used for aerating both light and heavy ingredients. It's especially good for cream and butter sauces.

hand-held electric mixer This good all-rounder gives you more control than a tabletop mixer and is far easier to use than a balloon whisk.

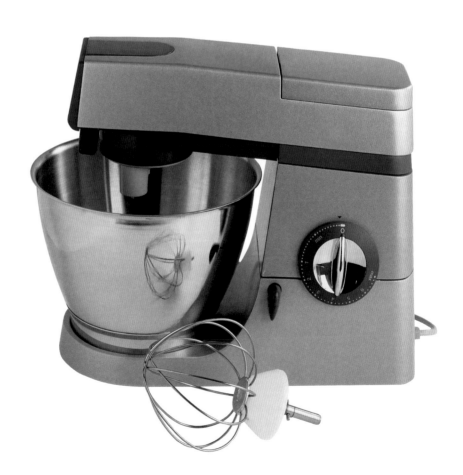

tabletop mixer
These super-powerful tabletop machines are great for cake mixes and for making meringues. Only for the serious cook, as they can be a little expensive.

ceramic bowl A traditional bowl finished with a white glaze is comfortable and easy to handle.

copper bowl A nonreactive copper bowl makes your meringue more stable and easier to work with.

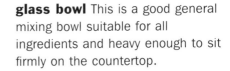

glass bowl This is a good general mixing bowl suitable for all ingredients and heavy enough to sit firmly on the countertop.

melamine bowl Practical, cheap and unbreakable, plastic-based bowls often have a nonslip rubber base.

stainless steel bowl Stainless steel is ideal for all food preparation as it is resistant to acid and colors.

cakes

cakes There are as many differerent ways of making cakes as there are cakes to make, but they're all based on the same core technique—whipping or whisking. The method and quantities of ingredients are then subtly altered to make the cake drier, moister, or lighter. Cake-making really is a fine art! In this chapter we show you the basic methods to make some of the most popular types of cake, plus some delicious variations.

american sponge the basic method The

technique of whipping or whisking is essential in the making of American sponge cakes. Try this traditional method to make a light, airy-textured cake.

step 1 Put the egg yolks into a large, roomy mixing bowl and add sugar. Whisk together using a hand-held electric mixer until the egg yolks are thick and pale yellow.

step 2 Remove the beaters and wash them. In a separate, roomy bowl, and with the clean beaters, start beating the egg whites, moving the beaters round the bowl.

step 3 Keep on beating the egg whites—you can use a balloon whisk instead of the electric mixer if preferred—until they reach the stiff peak stage.

step 4 Gradually whisk in the sugar, sprinkling it over the surface 1 tbsp. at a time, and making sure it is thoroughly incorporated before adding the next, until stiff and glossy.

step 5 Sift the flour over the egg yolks in the first bowl then fold it in carefully, using a spatula or large metal spoon, incorporating as much air as possible.

American whipped sponge cake

3 large eggs, separated • ½ cup sugar • 1 tsp. vanilla extract • ¼ tsp. cream of tartar • ⅓ cup all-purpose flour, sifted • pinch of salt • 1 cup whipping cream • ¼ lb. fresh strawberries • confectioners' sugar, for dusting

SERVES 6–8

This traditional American light-as-a-feather sponge cake recipe is flavored with vanilla and is perfect served with fruit and cream.

1. Preheat the oven to 350° F. Line the base of an 8-inch springform tube pan.

2. Whisk the egg yolks and add 4 tbsp. of the sugar together until thick and pale. Whisk in the vanilla extract.

3. Whisk the egg whites and cream of tartar until they are stiff. Gradually whisk in the remaining sugar until stiff and glossy. Sift the flour and salt over the egg yolks and fold in with a quarter of the whisked egg white. Fold in the remaining egg white.

4. Spoon the mixture into the prepared pan and bake until golden and the top springs back when pressed lightly, 30–40 minutes. Turn the pan upside down on a wire rack and let cool in the pan, 30 minutes. Run a knife around the inside of the pan then turn the cake out onto a wire rack. Turn right side up and let cool completely.

5. Whip the cream to soft peaks and pile onto the cake. Spread over the top and sides and decorate with small whole or halved strawberries. Dust the top with confectioners' sugar before serving.

Candied fruit cassata

6 tbsp. sweet Marsala • 2 cups fresh ricotta • scant 1 cup confectioners' sugar, sifted •
3 oz. unsweetened chocolate, finely chopped • ⅔ cup chopped mixed candied fruits •
½ cup toasted flaked almonds, chopped
For the ladyfingers • scant 1 cup all-purpose flour • 4 large eggs, separated • ½ cup
sugar • 1 tsp. vanilla extract • confectioners' sugar for dusting

SERVES 4–6

A *cassata*, or "little case" in Italian, is traditionally made in a loaf pan, but a bowl or straight-sided mold may also be used. A slightly drier, closer-textured ladyfinger is needed for this recipe, and to this end, the mixture contains a higher proportion of flour. Store-bought ladyfingers can be used—if you do this, miss out steps 1–4.

1. To make the ladyfingers, grease and flour two baking sheets. Preheat the oven to 350° F. Sift the flour into a bowl.

2. Put the egg yolks into a heatproof bowl. Put over a pan of simmering water and whisk with half the sugar until they reach the ribbon stage. Whisk in the vanilla extract.

3. In a separate bowl whisk the egg whites until they form stiff peaks. Add the remaining sugar and continue to whisk until they form a glossy meringue.

4. Use a large metal spoon to gently fold the meringue and then the sifted flour into the whisked egg yolks. Spoon the mixture into a piping bag fitted with a plain ¾-inch nozzle and quickly pipe 4½-inch lengths of mixture in lines on the prepared baking sheets. Dust the tops with confectioners' sugar and bake until pale golden and just firm to the touch, 15–18 minutes. Cool on a wire rack.

5. To assemble, line a 5-cup soufflé dish with plastic wrap. Cut half the ladyfingers into petal shapes to fit into the bottom. Dip into Marsala and arrange in the base. Cut the remaining fingers to fit around the sides and then dip each in the Marsala and arrange around the sides of the dish.

6. Mix remaining ingredients and spoon into the dish. Top with the leftover pieces and add the remaining Marsala. Cover and chill overnight. Turn out, dust with confectioners' sugar, and serve with cream.

Coffee, maple, and pecan sponge cake

½ cup all-purpose flour • pinch salt • 3 tbsp. unsalted butter • 3 large eggs • ⅓ cup
sugar • 1 tsp. instant coffee powder • 1 tbsp. hot water • ½ tsp. vanilla extract
For the frosting • ¾ cup butter • scant 1 cup confectioners' sugar • 4 tbsp. maple syrup •
1 tsp. instant coffee powder • 1 tbsp. hot water • 8 pecan halves to decorate

SERVES 6–8

**In this method, whole eggs are whisked with sugar over hot water until the ribbon stage
has been reached. The standard ratio is 2 tbsp. sugar and 2 tbsp. all-purpose flour for
each egg used. Melted butter is added to this cake mixture to increase richness and
also to improve its keeping properties.**

1. Grease and line an 8-inch round cake pan. Preheat the oven to 350° F. Sift the flour and salt
together three times and set aside. Melt the butter.

2. Break the eggs into a large bowl and add the sugar. Put over a pan of simmering water and whisk
together until they form the ribbon stage.

3. Dissolve the coffee powder in the hot water. Whisk in the coffee and vanilla extract. Sift the flour over
the eggs in three batches, drizzling a little butter around the bowl in between each batch and folding in.
Leave any white sediment left at the bottom of the saucepan.

4. Pour mixture into the prepared pan and bake until golden and the top springs back when pressed
lightly, 25–30 minutes. Let cool in the pan, 2–3 minutes, then turn out onto a wire rack to cool
completely.

5. For the frosting, beat the butter and sugar together until smooth. Dissolve coffee powder in the hot
water, then gradually beat into the frosting with the maple syrup until soft and smooth.

6. Cut the cake twice horizontally to make three layers and spread frosting over each layer. Assemble
the cake and spread remaining frosting around sides and on top. Decorate with pecans.

Chocolate and raspberry torte

⅓ cup all-purpose flour • 2 tbsp. cocoa • 3 tbsp. unsalted butter • 3 large eggs • ⅓ cup sugar • scant 2 cups whipping cream • 4 tbsp. orange liqueur • 6 oz. fresh or frozen raspberries • 1 tbsp. confectioners' sugar • 2 oz. unsweetened chocolate, grated

SERVES 6–8

This elegant gâteau makes a fantastic dessert as you can make it ahead of time and freeze to save time on the actual day.

1. Grease and line a 9-inch round cake pan. Preheat the oven to 350° F. Sift the flour and cocoa together and melt the butter.

2. Break the eggs into a large bowl and add the sugar. Place the bowl over a saucepan of hot water and whisk with a hand-held electric mixer until they reach the ribbon stage.

3. In three batches, sift the flour and cocoa over the eggs and fold in gently using a large metal spoon, drizzling a little butter around the bowl in between each batch. Leave any white sediment behind.

4. Pour mixture into the prepared pan and bake until brown and the top springs back when pressed lightly, 20 minutes. Let cool in the pan for 2–3 minutes, then turn out onto a wire rack to cool completely.

5. For the filling, whip the cream and orange liqueur until they form soft peaks. Fold in the raspberries, sugar, and grated chocolate.

6. Cut the cake through horizontally to make two layers. Line an 8-inch springform pan with waxed paper and trim the cake to fit the base of the pan. Put one of the sponge cake halves at the bottom. Pile in the raspberry cream and top with the remaining cake half. Press down evenly and freeze until the filling is firm, 4 hours. Dust the top with cocoa then remove from the pan and serve in slices.

Sponge cake roll with lemon cream

4 large eggs • ½ cup sugar, plus extra for dusting • scant 1 cup all-purpose flour •
1 cup mascarpone • 1 tsp. grated lemon peel • 1 tbsp. fresh lemon juice • 2 tbsp.
fresh orange juice • 4 tbsp. confectioners' sugar

SERVES 6

A ladyfinger batter (page 20) can also be used for sponge cake rolls but doesn't give such a moist cake. Jelly, butter-cream, or cream and fruit can be used for the filling too.

1. Preheat the oven to 425° F. Grease and line a 9 x 13-inch jelly roll pan with waxed paper.

2. Whisk the eggs and sugar with a hand-held electric mixer in a large bowl until thick and frothy and the beaters leave a trail when lifted out of the mixture—this is called the ribbon stage.

3. Sift and fold in the flour in three batches with a large metal spoon. Pour the mixture into the prepared pan and spread into the corners. Bake until golden brown and the top springs back when pressed lightly, about 10 minutes.

4. While the cake is cooking lay a sheet of waxed paper on a work surface and sprinkle liberally with sugar.

5. Holding the lining paper and pan edges, turn the cake out onto the paper. Peel the lining paper from the cake. Trim off the edges and score a cut 1-inch in from one of the shorter ends. Roll up cake with waxed paper and let cool on a wire rack.

6. Beat the filling ingredients together. Carefully unroll the jelly roll and spread with filling. Roll up and serve in slices.

Coconut and cherry sponge cake roll

4 large eggs • ½ cup sugar, plus extra for dusting • scant 1 cup all-purpose flour •
2 oz. piece creamed coconut, finely shredded
For the filling • ½ cup whipping cream • 2 tbsp. kirsch • ½ lb. pitted canned cherries,
drained

SERVES 6–8

Creamed coconut is available in 8-oz. packages at ethnic food stores (particularly West and East Indian food markets). It has a lovely flavor and is less granular than shredded. Use fresh cherries when they are in season.

1. Preheat the oven to 425° F. Grease and line a 9 x 13-inch jelly roll pan with waxed paper.

2. Whisk the eggs and sugar together in a large bowl with a hand-held electric mixer until they reach the ribbon stage. Sift the flour over the mixture in three batches and fold in gently after each addition with a large metal spoon. Fold in the creamed coconut with the last batch of flour.

3. Pour into prepared pan and spread lightly into corners. Bake until golden brown and the top springs back when pressed, 10 minutes.

4. While the cake is cooking lay a sheet of waxed paper on a work surface and sprinkle liberally with sugar.

5. Holding the lining paper and pan edges, turn the cake out onto the sugar-dusted paper. Peel the lining paper from the cake and trim the edges. Score a cut 1-inch in from one of the shorter ends.

6. Place a sheet of waxed paper over surface and roll up from scored end with the paper inside (see page 25). Cool on a wire rack.

7. Whip the cream and kirsch together until they form soft peaks. Unroll and fill cake. Add cherries and roll up. Serve sliced.

Middle Eastern orange cake

2 small oranges • 5 eggs • ⅔ cup brown sugar • 1½ cups ground almonds • ⅓ cup all-purpose flour • 1 tsp. baking powder • 2 tbsp. flaked almonds • confectioners' sugar, for dusting

SERVES 8–10

To flavor this moist and delicious cake, a whole orange, including the pith and peel, is used. This gives it a really intense citrus flavor that's perfect to serve as a dessert with sour cream or whipped cream.

1. Put the oranges in a saucepan and cover with water. Bring to a boil, cover and simmer until the oranges are really soft, 1½ hours. Drain and let cool. Halve the oranges and remove the pips then purée in a food processor or blender. Measure 1¼ cups of the pulp and discard the rest.

2. Grease and line a 9-inch round cake pan. Preheat the oven to 350° F. Whisk the eggs and sugar together in a large bowl until they are thick and foamy and the mixture leaves a ribbon trail when the whisk is lifted.

3. Fold the orange pulp into the eggs with the almonds, flour, and baking powder. Pour into the prepared pan, scatter the almonds over the surface, and bake 1 hour. Test for doneness by inserting a skewer into the center; it should come out clean if cooked.

4. Allow to cool in the pan, 10 minutes, then remove from the pan and peel off the lining paper. Cool on a wire rack or serve warm with whipped cream.

creamed sponge cake the basic method

These are notorious for separating. It helps to make sure all the ingredients are at room temperature before you start, which helps. Here butter and sugar are whipped or "creamed" together until light and fluffy to incorporate plenty of air. Add the eggs one at a time, getting yet more air into the cake mixture. This is the key to its success. The flour is folded in last to stop the cake from toughening. Proportions are generally equal weights but this can vary slightly.

step 1 Whisk the butter and sugar with a hand-held electric mixer or a balloon whisk in a large mixing bowl until they are pale and fluffy and no longer grainy.

step 2 Break the eggs into a separate bowl. Using a balloon whisk, beat the eggs to break them up slightly. This makes them easier to add to the rest of the mixture.

step 3 A little at a time, gradually whisk the beaten eggs into the butter and sugar mixture in the first bowl. Make sure you whisk well after each addition of egg.

step 4 Sift over the flour and any other ingredients like ground nuts. Fold into the mixture gently, with the electric mixer set at a slow speed, until thoroughly combined.

Orange and almond sponge cake

¾ cup butter • ⅔ cup sugar • 3 eggs • 1 cup self-rising flour • ⅓ cup ground almonds • a few drops almond extract

For the frosting • 10 oz. cream cheese (1¼ packages) • 2 tbsp. fresh orange juice • 2 tsp. grated orange peel • scant 1 cup confectioners' sugar, sifted • toasted flaked almonds and shredded orange peel to decorate

SERVES 6–8

This delicious moist sponge cake filled with cream cheese and flavored with tangy oranges is great with morning coffee and is special enough for dessert too.

1. Grease and line the bases of two 8-inch round layer pans. Preheat the oven to 375° F. Whisk the butter and sugar with a hand-held electric mixer in a bowl until they are pale and fluffy.

2. Whisk the eggs, then gradually whisk into the butter and sugar mixture. Sift over the flour and almonds and add the almond extract. Fold into the mixture gently until combined.

3. Spoon the mixture into the pans and level the surfaces. Bake until golden and the centers of the cakes spring back when pressed lightly, 20–25 minutes.

4. Turn out of the pans and cool on a wire rack. Meanwhile make the frosting. Beat the cream cheese in a bowl to soften. Add the orange juice, orange peel, and sugar, and beat until smooth and creamy.

5. Sandwich the cakes together with a little of the frosting, and use a palette knife to spread the rest of the frosting over the top. Scatter toasted flaked almonds and orange peel over the top to decorate.

Lemon and poppy seed pound cake

¾ cup butter • ⅔ cup sugar • 3 eggs, beaten • scant 1¼ cups self-rising flour •
1 tbsp. poppy seeds • 2 tsp. grated lemon peel
For the syrup • 3 tbsp. sugar • 1 lemon, juice only

SERVES 6–8

**This poppy seed cake is soaked with a tangy lemon syrup
after it's been baked to give a really moist, delicious
texture. It will keep well in an airtight container for up to
a week.**

1. Preheat the oven to 350°F. Grease and base line a 2 lb. loaf
pan.

2. Whip the butter and sugar together until light and fluffy.
Gradually whisk in the eggs a little at a time, then fold in the flour,
poppy seeds, and lemon peel.

3. Turn the mixture into the prepared pan and bake until risen,
golden, and a skewer inserted into the center comes out clean,
1¼–1½ hours. Remove the cake from the oven but leave in the
pan.

4. To make the syrup, gently heat the sugar and lemon juice
together until the sugar has dissolved. Bring to a boil then pour over
the cake and let cool. Cut into slices to serve.

Devil's food cake with chocolate orange frosting

6 oz. unsweetened chocolate • ⅝ cup unsalted butter • generous ½ cup sugar •
6 large eggs, separated • ½ cup all-purpose flour • ⅓ cup ground almonds
For the frosting • ⅔ cup whipping cream • 7 oz. unsweetened chocolate • 2 tsp. grated
orange peel

SERVES 8

This is a real chocoholic's dream. Wickedly indulgent, rich, and delicious. It combines the American sponge cake and creamed sponge cake methods.

1. Grease and line an 8-inch round cake pan with waxed paper. Preheat the oven to 350° F. Melt the chocolate for the cake in a bowl set over a pan of hot water. Cool slightly.

2. Meanwhile, beat butter and half the sugar until creamy. Beat in the melted chocolate then egg yolks, one at a time.

3. Sift the flour and almonds together into a separate bowl. Whisk the egg whites in a separate bowl until stiff, then gradually whisk in the remaining sugar. Stir half the egg whites into the chocolate mixture to loosen it slightly, then fold in the flour and almond mixture with the remaining egg white.

4. Spoon into the prepared pan and bake until a skewer inserted into the center comes out clean, 50–60 minutes. Cool in the pan, 10 minutes. Remove from the pan and cool completely on a wire rack.

5. To make the frosting, heat the cream in a saucepan until nearly boiling. Remove from the heat and stir in the chocolate until melted, then stir in the orange peel. Keep stirring until the frosting thickens. Pour over cake and spread evenly over the top and sides. Let the frosting set before dusting with confectioners' sugar.

Double chocolate chunk brownies

1 lb. 2 oz. unsweetened chocolate • 1 cup butter, diced • 1 tsp. instant coffee powder
1 tbsp. hot water • 3 large eggs • ⅔ cup sugar • 1 tsp. vanilla extract • scant 1 cup
self-rising flour • generous 1 cup pecan nuts, broken into pieces

MAKES 12 brownies

It's important when making brownies that they are not overcooked or they'll lose their characteristic delicious gooey center. Add any nuts you prefer, such as macadamia or peanut, but in my mind, pecans just go best of all with chocolate.

1. Preheat the oven to 375° F. Grease and line an 8 x 12-inch cake pan with waxed paper.

2. Chop 6 oz. of the chocolate into chunks and set aside. Put the rest in a bowl with the butter and melt slowly over a pan of hot water. Stir until smooth then let cool. Meanwhile, dissolve the coffee in the hot water.

3. Lightly whisk together the eggs, coffee, sugar, and vanilla. Gradually whisk in the chocolate and butter mixture, then fold in the flour, nuts, and chocolate chunks. Pour into the prepared pan. Bake until firm to the touch, 35–40 minutes.

4. Cool 5 minutes then cut into squares. Let cool in the pan before removing from the lining paper.

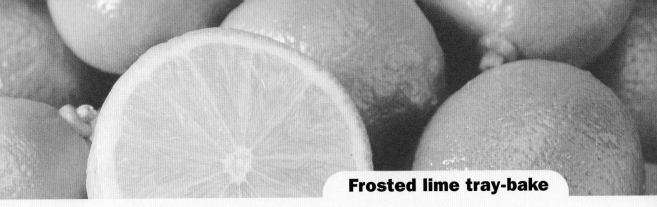

Frosted lime tray-bake

1 cup butter, softened • scant 1 cup sugar • 1½ cups self-rising flour • 1 tsp. baking powder • 4 large eggs • 2 tsp. grated lime peel

For the topping • 6 tbsp. fresh lime juice • scant ½ cup sugar • 4 tsp. grated lime peel

SERVES 6–8

This sponge cake uses a simple all-in-one method. It's a quick method that doesn't allow as much air to be incorporated as the traditional creaming method. To overcome this, extra rising agent is added with the flour. The crunchy topping is just as delicious if you use lemon or orange juice in place of the lime. The secret is to pour it over while the cake is still hot so the juice soaks in and the sugar forms a crunchy topping as it cools.

1. Preheat the oven to 350° F. Lightly grease and line a 7 x 11-inch baking tray with waxed paper.

2. Measure all the ingredients into a bowl and whisk together until light and smooth. Turn the mixture into the prepared pan and spread over evenly.

3. Bake until the cake is well risen, golden, and the top springs back when lightly pressed, 40 minutes.

4. While the cake is cooking, mix the topping ingredients together in a small bowl. Remove the cake from the oven and pour over the sugar topping. Let cool in the pan then turn out and remove the lining paper. Serve cut into squares.

Plum and amaretti sponge cake slice

¾ cup unsalted butter • ⅔ cup sugar • 3 large eggs • scant 1¼ cups self-rising flour, sifted • 2 tsp. grated lemon peel • 1 tbsp. fresh lemon juice • 3 plums, halved and pitted • 1 oz. amaretti cookies, coarsely crushed • 1 tbsp. coarse sugar, for sprinkling

SERVES 6

Crushed amaretti add an interesting crunch to this tray-bake and the almond flavor works incredibly well with the plums. Serve with sour cream or vanilla ice cream.

1. Grease and line a 6½ x 10-inch baking tray with waxed paper. Preheat the oven to 350° F.

2. Whip the butter and sugar together until pale and fluffy (see page 28). Add the eggs a little at a time whisking well after each addition. Sift the flour over the top and fold in with the lemon peel and juice.

3. Spoon into the prepared pan and spread into the corners. Arrange the plums, skin side up, over the top then sprinkle with the amaretti and sugar. Bake until risen and golden, 45–50 minutes.

4. Remove from the pan and let the cake cool on a wire rack before removing the lining paper.

Classic cheesecake with blackberry topping

14 graham crackers, crushed • 5 tbsp. butter, melted • 3 large eggs, separated • ⅔ cup sugar • 12 oz. cream cheese (1½ packages) • ⅔ cup sour cream • 2 tbsp. cornstarch • 2 tsp. vanilla extract • 4 tsp. grated lemon peel
For the topping • 1 lb. blackberries • ½ cup sugar • 4 tsp. arrowroot • 4 tbsp. blackberry or cherry liqueur

SERVES 6–8

You can't beat a classic cheesecake when it comes to pleasing everyone. This baked lemon version is topped with a blackberry glaze but it is just as delicious with any soft berry fruit of your choice. Raspberry and strawberry are especially good.

1. Preheat the oven to 350° F. Grease a 9-inch springform pan and line the base with waxed paper. Mix the crackers and butter together and press into the base of the pan.

2. Whisk the egg yolks and half the sugar until light and fluffy. Add the cream cheese a little at a time whisking until smooth. Mix in the sour cream, cornstarch, vanilla extract, lemon peel, and the remaining sugar.

3. In a separate, nonreactive bowl beat the egg whites until stiff, then fold them into the mixture. Pour into the pan and bake until just set and golden on top, 1–1¼ hours. Run a knife around the inside of the pan, then let cool in the oven with the door open slightly.

4. Meanwhile make the topping. Cook the blackberries in 4 tbsp. water until the juices run and the berries are soft, 5 minutes. Blend the arrowroot with the liqueur and stir into the fruit. Bring to a boil, then remove from the heat and set aside to cool.

5. Remove the cheesecake from the pan. Pour the blackberries and glaze over the top of the cheesecake. Chill 4 hours before serving.

Curd cheese tarts

For the pastry • scant 1 cup all-purpose flour • pinch salt • 5 tbsp. chilled butter, cut into pieces • 2 tbsp. sugar • ½ beaten egg • 1 tbsp. cold water
For the filling • 1 cup cottage cheese • 3 egg yolks • 2 tsp. grated lemon peel • 1 tsp. vanilla extract • ⅓ cup sugar • 4 tbsp. whipping cream • confectioners' sugar for dusting

MAKES 6 tarts

The filling for these little tartlets is enhanced with lemon peel. It's a kind of light cheesecake mixture cooked in individual pastry shells. Best served warm.

1. Put the flour, salt, and butter in a food processor and pulse until the mixture looks like fine bread crumbs. Add the sugar and pulse again to combine. Mix the egg and water together, then pour into the machine and pulse the mixture until it forms a ball. Wrap in plastic wrap and chill 30 minutes.

2. Preheat the oven to 400° F. Use the pastry to line six deep brioche pans and trim off any excess. Line each with waxed paper and baking beans and bake blind, 15 minutes. Remove the paper and beans and return to the oven, 5 minutes. Reduce the oven temperature to 325° F.

3. Put the cottage cheese, egg yolks, lemon peel, vanilla extract, and sugar in a bowl and whisk together until smooth. Lightly whisk in the cream until smooth. Pour into the pastry cases. Bake until lightly set, 25–30 minutes. Let cool slightly then serve dusted with confectioners' sugar.

angel food cake the basic method

angel food cake the basic method This classic cake uses just the egg whites in the cake mixture and has no fat added whatsoever, resulting in an extremely light and foamy sponge. It is cooked in a tube pan, left ungreased to encourage the mixture to cling to the sides as it rises. If it doesn't do this, you will have a cake which is sunk in the middle when you take it out of the oven. To help it even further, the cake is cooled upside down in the pan to really let it set.

step 1 Whisk the egg whites in a large bowl using a hand-held electric mixer, an egg whisk, or a balloon whisk, until the whites are just foamy, before they become stiff.

step 2 Add cream of tartar and salt at this stage, then continue beating the egg whites until they are stiff and form peaks when you lift up the beaters or whisk.

step 3 When the egg whites are at the stiff peak stage, gradually beat in the sugar, a spoonful at a time, until the egg whites are both stiff and glossy.

step 4 Add in the flour in three batches. Fold in each batch using a spatula or a large metal spoon, being careful to incorporate as much air as possible.

step 5 For the frosting, measure all the ingredients into a bowl, and put the bowl over a pan of hot water. Whisk with a hand-held electric mixer until thick.

Angel food cake

⅓ cup all-purpose flour • 1 tbsp. cornstarch • ⅔ cup plus 2 tbsp. sugar • 7 egg whites •
¾ tsp. cream of tartar • pinch of salt • 1 ½ tsp. vanilla extract
For the frosting • 2 egg whites • 1 ⅓ cups sugar • ¼ tsp. cream of tartar • 2 tbsp.
toasted chopped pistachios, plus extra to decorate

SERVES 6–8

**A truly magnificent feat of the art of cake-making, this
cake is held together almost purely by air.**

1. Preheat the oven to 350° F. Sift the flour and cornstarch
together. Add ⅓ cup of the sugar and sift together twice.

2. Whisk the egg whites until foamy. Add the cream of tartar and
salt and continue whisking until stiff.

3. Beat the remaining sugar into the egg whites until stiff and
glossy. Beat in the vanilla extract.

4. Fold in the flour then spoon mixture into a 9-inch springform
tube pan. The mixture should come up to the top of the pan.
Smooth over the top and bake until lightly golden on top and spongy
to the touch, 45–50 minutes. Remove from the oven and invert
onto a wire rack. Leave in the pan until cool.

5. For the frosting, put all the ingredients into a bowl, add 4 tbsp.
water, and put the bowl over a pan of hot water. Whisk with a hand-
held electric mixer until thick, 10–12 minutes.

6. Run a knife round the sides of the pan and remove. Spread the
frosting over the top. Finish with a sprinkle of pistachio nuts.

Strawberry ice-cream angel cake

⅓ cup all-purpose flour • 2 tbsp. cornstarch • ⅔ cup plus 2 tbsp. sugar • 7 large egg whites • ¾ tsp. cream of tartar • pinch salt • 1 ½ tsp. vanilla extract
For the filling • 4 tbsp. strawberry jelly • 2 cups strawberry ice cream • fresh strawberries, to serve

SERVES 6–8

A deliciously light sponge cake filled with strawberry ice cream makes a dreamy dessert and looks delicious. Remove from the freezer 30 minutes before serving and top with fresh strawberries for an extraspecial touch.

1. Preheat the oven to 350° F. Sift the flour and cornstarch together. Add just under half of the sugar and sift together twice.

2. Beat the egg whites in a nonreactive bowl until foamy. Add the cream of tartar and salt and continue beating until they are stiff.

3. Beat the remaining sugar into the egg whites a spoonful at a time until the egg whites form stiff peaks and are glossy. Beat in the vanilla extract.

4. Fold in the flour in three batches then spoon into a 9-inch springform tube pan. The mixture should come up to the top of the pan. Smooth over the top and bake until lightly golden on top and spongy to the touch, 45–50 minutes. Remove from the oven and invert onto a wire rack. Leave in the pan until cool.

5. Remove the cake from the pan and cool. Wash and dry the pan and line with waxed paper. Cut the cake through horizontally and return the base to the pan. Spread the jelly over the base and top with ice cream, spreading over evenly. Top with the other half and press down lightly. Freeze until firm. Serve topped with fresh strawberries.

Simple almond cake

1⅔ cups ground almonds • 2 tbsp. all-purpose flour, sifted • 7 large egg whites • ⅔ cup plus 2 tbsp. sugar • ½ cup whipping cream, whipped • 6 oz. strawberries, sliced • 2 tbsp. orange liqueur • confectioners' sugar for dusting

SERVES 6–8

This light moist cake is packed with ground almonds and is delicious with fresh fruit and cream. Choose whichever fruit you prefer and serve with fresh whipped cream for added luxury.

1. Preheat the oven to 350° F. Grease and line a 9-inch springform pan. Sift the almonds and flour together into a bowl and set aside. Whisk the egg whites in a nonreactive bowl until stiff. Keep whisking while gradually adding the sugar to form a stiff meringue.

2. Gently fold in the flour and almond mixture. Spoon into the pan and bake until golden and spongy to the touch, 25–30 minutes.

3. Cool in the pan then turn out and slice through horizontally. Drizzle the orange liqueur over each half. Spread one half with the whipped cream and top with the sliced strawberries. Top with the second half and dust with confectioners' sugar before serving.

Cappuccino truffle cake

1 tbsp. instant coffee powder • generous ½ cup hot water • 1½ cups no-need-to-soak pitted prunes, chopped • 4 tbsp. Tia Maria or other coffee liqueur • 6 oz. 70% cocoa solid unsweetened chocolate, broken into squares • ½ cup butter, plus extra for greasing • 5 eggs, separated • ½ cup sugar • 1 tsp. vanilla extract • 1 tbsp. cornstarch • cocoa for dusting • whipped cream to serve

SERVES 6–8

This wickedly delicious coffee and chocolate cake is more like a cold soufflé than a cake. Enjoy with an espresso coffee at the end of a meal.

1. Dissolve the coffee powder in the hot water, then pour over the prunes in a bowl with the Tia Maria. Let soak overnight.

2. Preheat the oven to 325° F. Grease and line a deep 8-inch springform pan with waxed paper.

3. The next day, melt the chocolate and butter together in a bowl set over a pan of hot water. Whisk the egg yolks and sugar with a hand-held electric mixer until they reach the ribbon stage. Stir in the vanilla extract, prunes, and melted chocolate mixtures and set aside.

4. With clean beaters, whisk the egg whites in a nonreactive bowl until stiff. Whisk in the cornstarch and fold into the chocolate mixture. Pour into the prepared pan and bake until springy to the touch, 50 minutes. Allow to cool in the pan.

5. Cut into slices and serve topped with a spoonful of whipped cream and a dusting of cocoa.

meringues

meringues
A meringue mixture is made by whipping together just two ingredients, egg whites and sugar, until stiff and glossy. Meringues can be shaped before baking (usually at a low temperature for a long time, to ensure the mixture is fully dried out) and served with fruit, cream, or other moist fillings. Some classic shapes are shown opposite. The mixture can also be heaped on top of a tangy fruit pie or incorporated into delectable cakes or macaroons.

meringue the basic method
When making a meringue mixture, the proportion of sugar should be 3 tbsp. to each egg white. A nonreactive copper bowl will produce the best foam with the greatest volume.

step 1 Whisk the egg whites to stiff peaks. Add half the sugar, 1 tbsp. at a time. Continue beating for 30 seconds. The meringue should be glossy and form short, soft peaks.

step 2 Fold in the rest of the sugar with a large metal spoon, carefully and thoroughly. The meringue should now be able to hold long stiff peaks when the whisk is lifted.

shaping meringues

quenelles Take two large metal spoons and scoop up some meringue with one of them. Scrape the meringue off onto the other spoon. Keep manipulating it between the two spoons until you have a smooth oval shape. Place on a baking sheet lined with waxed paper. Bake at 225° F, 3–4 hours.

fingers Fit a piping bag (plastic or made from waxed paper) with a large plain piping nozzle. Open out the top and stand in a tall jug. Spoon in the meringue and twist top to seal. Pipe into fingers on a baking sheet lined with waxed paper. Bake at 225° F, 3–4 hours.

nests Spoon meringue into a piping bag fitted with a large star or plain nozzle. Open out top and stand in a tall jug. Spoon in meringue and seal top. Pipe 4-inch circles in spirals onto a waxed paper-lined baking tray. Pipe more meringue around the edges of the circles to make "walls." Bake at 250° F, 1 hour.

Meringue nests

4 egg whites, at room temperature • ⅔ cup sugar • 1 tsp. vanilla extract • whipped
cream or sour cream • mixed berry fruits • confectioners' sugar for dusting

SERVES 4

**Filled with fruit and cream, these are a delight. Or if you
are feeling particularly wicked, you could try ice cream
and fudge sauce with extra cream on top.**

1. Preheat the oven to 250° F. Whisk the egg whites to stiff peaks.

2. Gradually whisk in half the sugar, then use a metal spoon to fold
in the remaining sugar. Fold in the vanilla extract.

3. Pipe the meringue into nests onto a baking tray lined with waxed
paper.

4. Bake 1 hour. Leave to cool on the trays. Fill with whipped cream
or sour cream, then top with mixed berry fruit and a dusting of
confectioners' sugar.

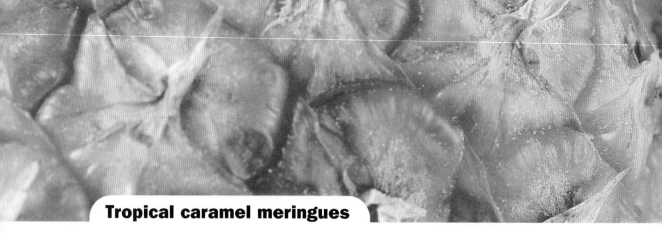

Tropical caramel meringues

For the meringue • **4 egg whites** • **scant ½ cup sugar** • **scant ½ cup golden brown sugar**
For the filling • **10 oz. cream cheese (1 ¼ packages)** • **1 ¼ cups confectioners' sugar** •
3 canned pineapple rings, drained well and finely chopped • **2 tsp. fresh lemon juice** •
2 peaches, pitted and sliced

MAKES 14 single meringues

**Using brown sugar in the meringue gives them a chewy
rich caramel flavor and fantastic golden color. Here
they've been filled with a pineapple frosting and peach
slices but coconut ice cream and raspberry sauce taste
good too.**

1. Preheat the oven to 225° F. Whisk the egg whites until stiff. Mix
the two sugars together and then add to the egg whites 1 tbsp. at a
time, beating well between each addition.

2. Line a baking sheet with waxed paper. Use 2 tablespoons to
shape the meringue into fourteen ovals (quenelles, see page 51).
Bake until thoroughly dried out, 3–4 hours.

3. Remove the meringues from the oven and let them cool on the
baking sheet.

4. To make the frosting, beat the cheese to soften it, then gradually
add the confectioners' sugar, beating well between each addition.
Stir in the pineapple and lemon juice.

5. Spoon some frosting onto half of the meringues, add a few slices
of peach and sandwich together with the remaining meringue halves.

Mixed berry basket

4 egg whites, at room temperature • ⅔ cup sugar • 1 tsp. vanilla extract
For the sauce • 6 oz. strawberries • 2 tbsp. confectioners' sugar •
For the filling • 1 cup mascarpone cheese • 1 cup whipping cream •
3 tbsp. Cointreau or other orange liqueur • ¾ lb. mixed berry fruits

SERVES 4

**Use a plain meringue mixture to make a tray or basket
and fill with any fruit of your choice. Here it is filled with
a mixture of berries with a fragrant strawberry sauce
drizzled over the top.**

1. Line a baking sheet with waxed paper. Preheat the oven to
275° F. Whisk the egg whites until stiff. Add the sugar 1 tbsp. at a
time, until nearly all the sugar has been added.

2. Continue beating until glossy peaks form, 30 seconds. Use a
metal spoon to fold in the remaining sugar, then fold in the vanilla
extract.

3. Spoon half the meringue onto the baking sheet and spread out
to a 7 x 11-inch rectangle. Either pipe a rope edge or small
rosettes around the sides on top of the meringue base or drop
small spoonfuls onto the edges to form a border. Bake 1 hour.
Reduce the oven temperature to 225° F and continue cooking until
the meringue is lightly colored and crisp to the touch, 2–2½ hours.
Let cool on the tray, then run a palette knife underneath and
transfer to a flat plate.

4. To make the sauce, purée the strawberries and confectioners'
sugar in a blender or food processor, then sieve to remove the pips.
Whip the mascarpone and cream together and stir in the Cointreau.
Spoon into the meringue basket and top with the prepared fruits.
Drizzle over some of the sauce to serve.

Raspberry and passionfruit pavlova

4 egg whites • scant 1 cup sugar • 1 tsp. white wine vinegar • 1 ½ tsp. cornstarch • 1 tsp. vanilla extract
For the topping • 2 ½ cups whipping cream • ¾ lb. fresh raspberries • 4 passionfruit • fresh mint sprigs • confectioners' sugar for dusting   **SERVES 4–6**

This marshmallow-like meringue is believed to have been created in Australia in the 1930s to celebrate the visit of the ballerina Anna Pavlova. It can be topped with any fruit you like.

1. Preheat the oven to 350° F. Line a baking tray with waxed paper. Whisk the egg whites until stiff. Whisk in the sugar 1 tbsp. at a time, whisking well between each addition.

2. Blend the vinegar, cornstarch, and vanilla extract together in a small bowl, then whisk into the meringue mixture.

3. Spoon the mixture onto the paper lined baking tray and spread out to a 10-inch circle. Make a slight dip in the center. Bake for 5 minutes. Reduce the oven temperature to 300° F. Bake until firm to the touch and lightly golden, an additional 1¼ hours. Turn off the oven and let cool in the oven, 2–3 hours.

4. Slide a palette knife under the pavlova and transfer to a flat serving plate. Whip the cream until it forms soft peaks and spoon into the center of the pavlova.

5. Scatter the raspberries over the top. Scoop the seeds and pulp out of the passionfruit, then scatter onto the raspberries. Decorate with mint and dust with confectioners' sugar.

Double chocolate mini alaskas

5 oz. graham crackers or chocolate-coated grahams, crushed • 3 tbsp. butter, melted • scant 2 cups good quality dairy chocolate chip ice cream • 1 flaked chocolate bar, cut into four • 3 egg whites • ⅔ cup sugar • ½ tsp. vanilla extract
cocoa for dusting   MAKES 4

These have a cookie base for simplicity in place of the more usual cake base. Use the best quality ice cream you can find as it needs to freeze really firmly before being baked—soft serve won't do. Italian-style cooked meringue is more stable than the usual cold whipped method so it can withstand cold and then hot.

1. Mix the crushed graham crackers with the melted butter. Place a 3¼-inch round cookie cutter on a greased baking sheet and spoon a quarter of the crumbs into it. Press down well, then remove the cutter. Repeat three times to make four bases.

2. Place the tray in a freezer to firm up, 30 minutes. Soften the ice cream slightly then spoon some onto each of the bases. Top each with a piece of flaked chocolate. Return to the freezer and leave until solid, 1–2 hours.

3. Whisk egg whites, sugar, and vanilla extract until frothy. Place the bowl over a pan of gently simmering water and continue whisking until the meringue is thick and glossy, 10 minutes. Remove from the heat and continue whisking until cool.

4. Take the bases out of the freezer and cover completely with the meringue. Return to the freezer and freeze, at least 4 hours.

5. Preheat the oven to 425° F. Bake until golden, 6–8 minutes. Dust with cocoa before serving.

Hazelnut meringue cake

4 egg whites • scant 1 cup sugar • 1 tsp. vanilla extract • 1 tsp. cider vinegar •
1 tsp. cornstarch • ⅔ cup finely ground toasted hazelnuts • 2 tbsp. toasted coarsely
chopped hazelnuts
For the filling • ⅔ cup plain yogurt • 2 tbsp. bourbon • 2 tbsp. honey • ½ cup whipping
cream • ½ lb. raspberries • confectioners' sugar, for dusting   **SERVES 6–8**

**This rich crumbly hazelnut meringue is filled with a
bourbon-laced cream and fresh raspberries and would
make a wonderfully impressive dessert to serve at a
dinner party. Fill about an hour before serving—any
longer and the meringue will start to go soft.**

1. Preheat the oven to 350° F. Grease and line the bases of two
8-inch round layer cake pans with waxed paper.

2. Whisk the egg whites until stiff. Gradually whisk in the sugar until
it forms a stiff glossy meringue. Fold in the vanilla extract, vinegar,
cornstarch, and ground hazelnuts.

3. Divide the mixture between the two pans and spread evenly.
Scatter the chopped hazelnuts over the top of one, then bake until
crisp, 50–60 minutes. Remove from the pans and cool on a wire
rack.

4. While the meringues are cooling make the raspberry cream. Stir
the yogurt, bourbon, and honey together, whip the cream until it
forms soft peaks, then fold into the yogurt with the raspberries.
Sandwich the two meringues together with the cream, with the nut-
topped one on top. Dust with confectioners' sugar before serving.

Lemon-lime meringue pie

¾ lb. ready-made pie crust dough • 2 tbsp. grated lime peel • 6 tbsp. fresh lime juice
2 tbsp. grated lemon peel • 6 tbsp. fresh lemon juice • generous ½ cup sugar •
5 tbsp. cornstarch • 4 tbsp. butter • 5 egg yolks • confectioners' sugar for dusting
For the meringue • 5 egg whites • 1 cup sugar • ½ tsp. vanilla extract • 1 tsp. cider
vinegar • 1 tsp. cornstarch

SERVES 6–8

**Tangy, sweet, and delicious, this deep pie will have
everyone coming back for more. Good chilled too.**

1. Roll out the pastry on a lightly floured surface and use to line a
deep 9-inch loose-bottomed tart pan. Prick the base and chill 10
minutes. Preheat the oven to 400° F. Line the pastry case with
waxed paper and baking beans and bake blind, 15 minutes.
Remove the paper and beans and return to the oven, 5 minutes.
Reduce oven temperature to 300° F.

2. Make up the lime and lemon juices in a cup to scant 1 cup with
water if necessary. Pour into a saucepan with the peel and add a
scant 1 cup water and sugar. Heat gently to dissolve sugar.

3. Mix the cornstarch with 5 tbsp. cold water. Whisk the cornstarch
mixture into the juice. Continue whisking gently until thickened, then
whisk in the butter and egg yolks. Bring to a boil over a low heat
whisking all the time then simmer, 3 minutes. Remove from the
heat and set aside to cool slightly. Pour into the pastry case.

4. Whisk the egg whites until stiff. Gradually whisk in the sugar until
glossy. Blend the vanilla extract, vinegar, and cornstarch together
and fold into the meringue.

5. Place spoonfuls over the pie. Bake until lightly golden, 40–50
minutes. Allow to cool, 20 minutes, before serving.

Strawberry and pistachio vacherin

4 egg whites • ⅔ cup sugar • 4 tbsp. golden brown sugar • ⅓ cup toasted,
finely chopped pistachio nuts • **For the filling** • 1 cup whipping cream •
2 tbsp. confectioners' sugar • 2 tbsp. coconut rum •
To decorate • ½ lb. strawberries • fresh mint leaves

SERVES 4

**A vacherin is a cold meringue dessert, named for the
wheel of cheese it resembles. Finely chopped pistachios
flavor this meringue mixture and also give it a lovely
chewy nutty center. Make sure the meringue is really
thick and glossy before folding in the nuts.**

1. Preheat the oven to 275° F. Line two baking trays with waxed
paper and draw an 8-inch circle on each sheet. Turn them over so
the pencil is on the underside.

2. Whisk the egg whites until stiff. Mix the sugars together, then
add to the egg whites a spoonful at a time until all the sugar has
been added. Fold in the nuts.

3. Spoon the meringue into a piping bag fitted with a plain nozzle.
Pipe the meringue in a spiral, starting from the center of each
circle, to make two circles. Bake until crisp to the touch and lightly
colored, 1–2 hours. Let cool in the turned off oven, then carefully
peel off the paper.

4. Make the filling by whipping the cream, confectioners' sugar,
and rum together until it forms soft peaks. Spread three quarters of
the cream over one meringue circle. Top with some sliced
strawberries and then the other meringue.

5. Top with spoonfuls of the cream and finish with halved
strawberries and mint leaves.

Chocolate and chestnut macaroon cake

2 cups confectioners' sugar • ½ tsp. baking soda • 4 large egg whites • generous 1 cup ground almonds • For the filling • scant ½ cup chestnut purée • 2 tbsp. maple syrup • 3 oz. unsweetened chocolate • 1 cup mascarpone cheese • ½ cup whipping cream • chocolate curls, to decorate

SERVES 6–8

This three layered almond meringue cake is filled with a rich chestnut and chocolate-flavored cream. To give it an extra special finish each serving can be drizzled thinly with melted dark chocolate. Chestnut purée is available at gourmet specialty stores.

1. Line three baking sheets with waxed paper and draw a 7-inch circle on each. Preheat the oven to 275° F. Sift the confectioners' sugar and baking soda together.

2. Whisk the egg whites until stiff. Gradually beat in three-quarters of the confectioners' sugar until it is stiff and glossy. Mix the rest into the ground almonds and fold into the whites. Divide the mixture between the three circles and spread out evenly. Bake for 10 minutes. Reduce the oven temperature to 225° F and cook, an additional 1¼ hours. Cool on a wire rack then peel away the paper.

3. Beat the chestnut purée and maple syrup together until smooth. Melt the chocolate in a bowl set over a pan of hot water. Stir the melted chocolate into the chestnut purée, then beat in the mascarpone followed by the cream.

4. Place a meringue circle on a plate and spread with half of the chestnut mixture. Place a second meringue on top and spread that with the remaining chestnut mixture. Top with the remaining meringue round. Decorate the top with chocolate curls.

Almond macaroons

2 egg whites • ⅓ cup ground almonds • ⅔ cup sugar • 2 tbsp. semolina or ground rice •
a few drops of almond extract • 4 oz. unsweetened chocolate chips • whole blanched
almonds, to decorate

MAKES 12 macaroons

**Macaroons are traditionally made on edible rice paper, but
if you have trouble finding it, then waxed paper is fine
(although you won't be able to eat it of course).**

1. Preheat the oven to 325° F. Line two baking sheets with rice paper.

2. Mix the almonds, sugar, and semolina. In a separate bowl, whisk
the egg whites with a handheld electric mixer until stiff.

3. Gradually fold in the sugar and almond mixture until quite stiff.

4. Fold in the chocolate chips. Place tablespoonfuls of the mixture
onto the trays, leaving spaces between them. Place an almond on
top of each one and bake until golden brown, 15–20 minutes. Cool,
then tear the rice paper between each cookie, or peel off if you're
using waxed paper.

Blueberry and white chocolate meringue roll

1 cup sugar • ½ vanilla bean • 5 egg whites • confectioners' sugar for dusting
For the filling • 5 oz. white chocolate • 1 cup mascarpone cheese • ½ cup plain yogurt •
4 oz. blueberries

SERVES 6

This is rather an unusual idea using a meringue mixture to create a roulade-type dessert. The filling is a white chocolate cream with tangy fragrant blueberries throughout.

1. Preheat the oven to 425° F. Grease and line a 9 x 13-inch jelly roll pan with waxed paper.

2. Combine the sugar and the seeds from inside the vanilla bean. Whisk the egg whites until stiff. Gradually whisk in the vanilla sugar a spoonful at a time until it forms a stiff glossy meringue.

3. Spread the meringue mixture into the prepared pan and bake, 8 minutes. Lower the oven temperature to 325° F and continue cooking until firm to the touch, 10 minutes.

4. Remove the meringue from the oven and turn out onto a sheet of waxed paper dusted with confectioners' sugar. Remove the paper from the base and let cool, 10 minutes.

5. Meanwhile, make the filling. Melt the chocolate in a bowl set over hot water. Stir in the yogurt, then beat into the mascarpone. Spread the cream over the meringue and top with the blueberries. Roll up from one of the long sides using the paper underneath to help. Leave wrapped in the paper at least 1 hour before serving.

ice creams and other desserts

ice creams and other desserts

Smooth, creamy ice cream is everyone's favorite comfort food. It's easier to make than you think—you don't even need a specialized ice cream maker—and the possibilities for different and delicious flavorings are endless. This chapter also features a selection of miscellaneous desserts that use whipping techniques—trifles, sorbets, mousses, and that sublime Italian creation, zabaglione.

ice cream the basic method

An ice cream base is made by combining a custard mixture with whipped cream. It's frozen for short bursts and whisked to break down the ice crystals formed during freezing.

step 1 Remove the vanilla bean from the heated milk. Whisk the egg yolks and sugar with a hand-held electric mixer until pale and thick. Lightly whisk in the hot milk.

step 2 Pour into a heavy-based pan. Cook over low heat, stirring constantly until the mixture thickens to the consistency of heavy cream and coats the back of a spoon.

step 3 Tear off some plastic wrap and then press down gently over the surface of the custard (this will stop a skin from forming) and set to one side to cool.

step 4 Pour the whipping cream into a bowl. Using a hand-held electric mixer, whip the cream until it forms stiff peaks. When the custard is cold, fold in the cream.

step 5 Pour into a freezer container and freeze until half-frozen, (or churn in an ice-cream maker). Whisk to break up ice crystals. Repeat twice more until thick. Stir in flavorings and, finally, freeze until firm.

Blue lagoon ice cream

generous ½ cup milk • ½ vanilla bean • 2 egg yolks • 5 tbsp. sugar • ½ lb. blueberries • 1 tbsp. white rum • 1 cup whipping cream • 1 ½ oz. store-bought meringues

SERVES 6

If you want to make plain vanilla ice cream, omit the blueberry sauce and meringues and freeze. Or, if you want to use any other fruit or chocolate sauce, swirl them in at the end.

1. Bring the milk and vanilla bean to simmering point over low heat. Remove the vanilla bean and remove the pan from the heat. Whisk the egg yolks and 4 tbsp. of the sugar with a hand-held electric mixer until pale and thick, then lightly whisk in the milk.

2. Return to a clean heavy-based saucepan. Cook over low heat, stirring continuously until the mixture thickens. Cover with plastic wrap and let cool. Meanwhile, cook the blueberries with the rest of the sugar and 1 tbsp. water until broken up, 2 minutes. Cool then stir in the rum.

3. Whip the cream and fold into the custard. Pour into a shallow freezer-proof container and freeze until half-frozen, about 2–3 hours (or churn in an ice-cream maker), then beat with a hand-held electric mixer. Repeat this process at least twice more until thick.

4. Swirl the meringues through the ice cream followed quickly by the blueberry sauce, to make a marbled pattern. Spoon into a freezerproof container and freeze until firm. Remove from the freezer 20–30 minutes before serving.

Coffee and maple ice cream

½ cup milk • ½ vanilla bean • 2 egg yolks • 2 tbsp. sugar • 2 tbsp. instant coffee
3 tbsp. maple syrup • 1 cup whipping cream • 2 tbsp. coarsely chopped pecan nuts

SERVES 6

**This ice cream is flavored with an unbeatable
combination of coffee and maple syrup and has pieces of
pecan stirred through to give an irresistible crunch.**

1. Heat the milk and vanilla bean together over a low heat until the
milk almost boils. Remove from the heat and remove the vanilla
bean. Whisk the egg yolks and sugar together until pale and thick,
then whisk in the milk.

2. Return the mixture to a heavy-based nonstick saucepan. Cook
over a low heat, stirring continuously until the mixture thickens to
the consistency of whipping cream. Stir in the coffee and maple
syrup until the coffee granules have dissolved. Cover the surface of
the mixture with plastic wrap and let cool.

3. Whip the cream until it forms soft peaks. Fold into the custard.
Pour the mixture into a container, place in the freezer until half-
frozen, about 2–3 hours (or churn in an ice-cream maker), and
whisk to break up the ice crystals. Repeat this process twice more.

4. When almost fully frozen, swirl in the pecans. Spoon into a
freezerproof container and freeze until firm. Remove from the
freezer 20–30 minutes before serving.

Black currant and white rum fool

1 lb. fresh or frozen black currants • 4 tbsp. sugar • 2 tbsp. fresh orange juice • 2 tbsp. white rum • 1 cup whipping cream, lightly whipped
For the custard • ½ cup milk • ½ vanilla bean • 2 egg yolks • 4 tbsp. sugar

SERVES 4

A fool is a combination of puréed fruit, custard, and whipped cream and in fact, it's not unlike an unfrozen ice-cream mixture. Tart fruit seem to work best, so use fruits such as rhubarb, gooseberries, plums, or, as here, black currants.

1. Make a fruit purée by cooking the black currants, sugar, and orange juice in a covered pan until very soft, 5 minutes. Let cool then purée in a food processor or blender. Push the juice and pulp through a sieve. Stir in the white rum and set aside.

2. For the custard, heat the milk and vanilla bean together over a low heat until the milk almost boils. Remove from the heat and remove the vanilla bean. Whisk the egg yolks and sugar together until pale and thick, then whisk in the milk.

3. Return the mixture to a heavy-based nonstick saucepan. Cook over a low heat stirring continuously until the mixture thickens to the consistency of whipping cream. Cover the surface with plastic wrap and let cool.

4. Stir the black currant purée into the custard and then gently fold in the whipped cream. Stir gently until it thickens slightly then spoon into glasses and chill before serving.

Candied fruit bombe

4 tbsp. dark rum or brandy • 1 cup mixed dried fruit, e.g., apricots, raisins, figs, cherries, and cranberries, chopped • 1 cup milk • 1 vanilla bean • 2 egg yolks • 4 tbsp. sugar • 1 cup whipping cream • 2 oz. unsweetened chocolate, grated • fresh figs and mint sprigs to serve

SERVES 6

You can make this weeks ahead, so it's really great for entertaining. If you want to make it even easier on yourself, use a good quality ready-made vanilla pudding instead of the egg custard in the recipe.

1. Pour rum or brandy over the fruit and soak overnight. The next day heat the milk and vanilla bean to simmering point over low heat. Remove from the heat. Whisk the egg yolks and sugar with a hand-held electric mixer until pale, then whisk in the hot milk.

2. Return to a clean heavy-based nonstick saucepan. Cook over low heat, stirring continuously with a wooden spoon until the mixture thickens to the consistency of whipping cream. Cover the surface of the mixture with plastic wrap and set aside to cool. Remove vanilla.

3. Lightly whip the cream until it forms soft peaks then fold into the custard. Freeze in a shallow freezerproof container until half-frozen, about 2–3 hours (or churn in an ice-cream maker), then stir until it holds its shape. Repeat this process at least twice more. Mix the rum-soaked fruits into the half frozen mixture with the chocolate.

4. Spoon into a plastic wrap-lined 2 lb. pudding mold or six individual molds. Freeze until firm. Remove from the freezer 30 minutes before serving. Turn out and remove the plastic wrap. Serve with fresh figs and fresh mint sprigs.

Caribbean coconut trifle

¾ lb. sweet pineapple flesh • 1 cup whipping cream • 4 tbsp. coconut milk • ⅔ cup sour cream • 4 tbsp. confectioners' sugar • 2 papaya, peeled, seeded, and chopped • 2 mangoes, peeled, pitted, and chopped • 2 tbsp. fresh lime juice • toasted flaked coconut, to decorate

SERVES 6

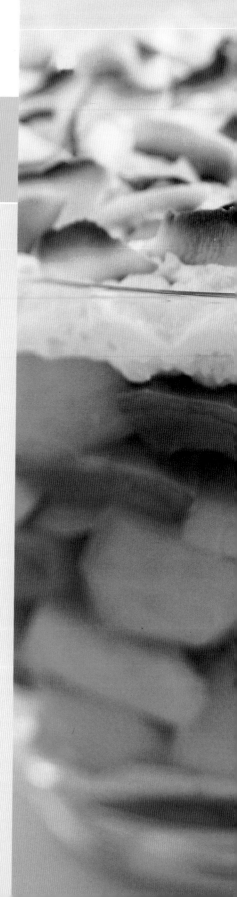

This trifle is actually based on a Caribbean fruit fool—fruit stirred into thick vanilla-flavored cream. Canned coconut milk is used in Thai cooking and is now available in many supermarkets.

1. Cut the pineapple into large chunks, put in a food processor or blender, and process briefly until chopped. Tip into a sieve and let the juice drain away.

2. Whip the whipping cream until it forms soft peaks, then lightly fold in the coconut milk, sour cream, and confectioners' sugar.

3. Fold the drained pineapple into the cream mixture. Put the papaya and mango in a large serving bowl and pour over the lime juice and 4 tbsp. of the drained pineapple juice.

4. Spoon the pineapple cream on top of the fruit and scatter over the toasted coconut flakes.

right: Caribbean coconut trifle

Kahlua and chocolate trifle

½ cup strong fresh coffee • 4 tbsp. Kahlua or other coffee liqueur •
6 oz. ladyfingers (see page 20) • ⅓ cup sugar • 2 tsp. vanilla
extract • 2 cups mascarpone cheese • 1 cup whipping cream •
4 oz. unsweetened chocolate, grated • cocoa, to serve

SERVES 4–6

**This is based on the Italian tiramisu, which is traditionally
flavored with coffee and laced with liqueur. Kahlua gives
the fresh coffee a bit of a kick.**

1. Grease and line a 2 lb. loaf pan with plastic wrap. Mix the coffee
and Kahlua together. Dip the ladyfingers into the mixture and use
some to line the base of the pan.

2. Whisk the sugar and vanilla extract into the mascarpone. Add
the cream a little at a time whisking on a slow speed until smooth.

3. Spoon half of the mixture on top of the ladyfingers in the pan
and spread over evenly. Add half the grated chocolate, then repeat
a layer of the dipped ladyfingers, the remaining creamed mixture,
grated chocolate, and a final layer of dipped ladyfingers. Drizzle any
remaining coffee mixture over the top.

4. Cover with a layer of plastic wrap then chill, 2–3 hours. Remove
from the pan and peel off the plastic wrap. Dust with a generous
amount of cocoa, slice, and serve.

Lychee sorbet

6 tbsp. sugar • 14-oz. can lychees in syrup • 1 tbsp. elderflower cordial • 1 egg white

SERVES 6

Elderflower cordial adds a wonderful, scented flavor to this simple refreshing sorbet, but if it's hard to find, freshly made lemonade will have a similar effect. Whipped egg whites are added to lighten.

1. Heat the sugar and 1 cup water together until the sugar has dissolved. Bring to a boil and simmer 1 minute. Remove from the heat and let cool.

2. Purée the lychees and syrup in a food processor or blender then pass through a sieve, pressing down well to extract all the juice. Add the elderflower cordial.

3. Pour the mixture into a shallow freezerproof container and freeze until soft but just beginning to hold its shape, about 2–3 hours.

4. Whisk the egg white until it forms soft peaks then add to the half-frozen sorbet mixture. Continue freezing and whisking by hand twice more until it becomes thick and creamy. Freeze until required.

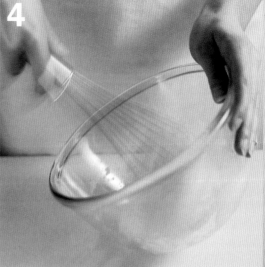

5. Remove from the freezer and put in the refrigerator 5–10 minutes before serving.

Chilled mandarin and lemon mousse

2 tsp. grated lemon peel · 2 tbsp. fresh lemon juice · 2 tsp. grated mandarin orange peel · 8 tbsp. fresh mandarin orange juice · 1 package powdered gelatin · 4 eggs, separated · ½ cup sugar · 1 cup whipping cream · whipped cream, to decorate · pared lemon and mandarin peel, to decorate

MAKES 6 SMALL GLASSES

This fresh, fruity summer dessert looks so pretty decorated with little twists of lemon and mandarin peel.

1. Put the fruit peel in a bowl. Measure the fruit juice—it should be no more than 1 cup. Pour the measured juice into a small saucepan and sprinkle the gelatin in. Let soak for 5 minutes, then heat gently without boiling until the gelatin has dissolved. Let cool.

2. Add the egg yolks and sugar to the fruit peel and whisk until the mixture is very thick and creamy.

3. With clean beaters, whisk the egg whites until stiff and whip the cream until it forms soft peaks. Gently whisk the gelatin mixture into the yolks, then fold in the cream and finally the egg whites.

4. Spoon the mixture into glasses and chill until set, 3–4 hours. Decorate with whipped cream and lemon and mandarin peel.

Note: Recipes using raw eggs should be avoided by infants, the elderly, pregnant women, and anyone with a compromised immune system.

Rich mocha pots

6 oz. unsweetened chocolate, broken into pieces • 3 tbsp. strong black coffee • 1 tbsp. butter • 4 eggs, separated • 2 tbsp. brandy • 4 tbsp. confectioners' sugar • whipped cream, to decorate • grated chocolate or curls, to decorate

MAKES 6–8 pots

This dark, sultry take on chocolate mousse is a sophisticated, grown-up dessert. For best results use the finest chocolate you can find and chill the mousse well before serving.

1. Melt the chocolate in a bowl set over a pan of hot water. Stir in the coffee and butter until smooth. Remove from the heat and whisk in the egg yolks one by one until the mixture is smooth and glossy. Whisk in the brandy then set aside to cool and thicken slightly while you are whisking the egg whites.

2. Whisk the egg whites in a nonreactive bowl until stiff. Gradually add the sugar and continue whisking until glossy and thick. Fold into the cooled chocolate mixture.

3. Pour into six or eight small teacups or professional ramekins and chill until firm, 3–4 hours. Top with whipped cream and the grated chocolate or chocolate curls.

Note: Recipes using raw eggs should be avoided by infants, the elderly, pregnant women, and anyone with a compromised immune system.

Creamy zabaglione

4 egg yolks • 4 tbsp. sugar • ½ cup Marsala • 1 tsp. grated lemon peel • ½ cup whipping cream, whipped • ½ tsp. vanilla extract • ladyfingers or biscotti to serve

SERVES 4

Beating over hot water warms up the mixture and lets the egg yolks cook and thicken the mixture. Take care though—if it overheats, it will separate.

1. Put the egg yolks and sugar into a bowl and whisk over simmering water with a hand-held electric mixer until the mixture is pale yellow, creamy, and smooth.

2. Add the Marsala a little at a time, whisking constantly until the mixture is very light and almost thick enough to leave a trail when the beaters are lifted.

3. Remove the bowl from the heat and whisk, an additional 5 minutes. Fold in the lemon peel, whipped cream, and vanilla extract and serve in glasses with ladyfingers or biscotti to dip in.

Seared fruit in frothy orange sauce

2 fresh figs · ½ sweet pineapple, peeled and cored · 1 ripe mango · 6 oz. blackberries · 4 tbsp. white wine · ⅓ cup sugar · 6 egg yolks · 2 tbsp. Cointreau or other orange liqueur

SERVES 4

This out-of-the-ordinary gratin is strictly for adults. A colorful combination of island fruits are covered with a frothy egg based sauce flavored with orange liqueur.

1. Cut the figs into wedges and the pineapple into chunks. Peel the mango, cut the flesh off the stone, and then into chunky pieces.

2. Divide the prepared fruit between four individual gratin dishes and scatter the blackberries over the top.

3. Heat the wine and sugar in a saucepan until the sugar has dissolved. Cook 5 minutes.

4. Put the egg yolks in a large heatproof bowl. Place over a pan of simmering water and whisk the yolks until they are pale, thick, and fluffy. Slowly pour the syrup into the egg yolks, with the Cointreau, whisking all the time until it thickens.

5. Spoon the frothy mixture over the fruit and place under a hot broiler on a low shelf until the topping is golden. Serve immediately.

Cherry syllabub

½ cup sweet white wine • 4 tbsp. white or coconut rum • 2 tbsp. fresh lemon juice • generous ⅓ cup sugar • scant 2 cups whipping cream • 10 oz. fresh pitted cherries • crisp almond biscuits, to serve

SERVES 4

The joy of this dessert is that any flavored liqueur or spirit of your choice can be added to the basic mixture. Also the fruit can be varied depending on the season and your preference.

1. In a large bowl combine the white wine, rum, lemon juice, and sugar, and mix well until the sugar has dissolved.

2. Stir in the cream and then whip until stiff enough to hold soft peaks. Spoon the cherries into the bases of four glasses and top with the cream syllabub.

3. Serve immediately with crisp almond cookie to dip into the cream. If left to stand for too long the mixture will separate out again.

soufflés

soufflés

Soufflé is a French word which literally means "puffed up." In cooking it's used to describe a light, frothy dish, just stiff enough to hold its shape. Whether sweet or savory, soufflés should be firm on the outside and deliciously wobbly in the center. This chapter also includes roulades—sophisticated-looking, rolled-up variations on the classic soufflé—and soufflé omelets, which are so much lighter and fluffier than standard omelets.

soufflés the basic method

The classic soufflé is made by mixing a thick, flavored sauce, with flour and butter as its base, with whisked egg whites, which expand in a hot oven to give the soufflé its puffy appearance.

step 1 Melt the butter in a large saucepan, add the flour, and cook for 1 minute. Whisk in the milk then bring to a boil, stirring, until the sauce has thickened.

step 2 Remove from the heat and add flavorings. Let the mixture cool for a few minutes. Whisk in the egg yolks one at a time until the sauce is smooth and glossy.

step 3 With clean beaters and in a separate bowl, whisk the egg whites until stiff but not dry. This is just before they reach the stiff peak stage.

step 4 Take a large spoonful of the whisked egg whites and beat it into the flavored sauce base to slacken it a bit. Then gently fold in the rest of the whisked egg whites.

step 5 Pour the mixture into a soufflé dish. Run your finger around the top inside edge of the dish. When the soufflé is baked, this is what gives it its little "cap."

Cheese soufflé

¼ cup butter, plus extra for greasing • ⅓ cup all-purpose flour • 1 cup milk • 5 eggs, separated • pinch of fresh grated nutmeg • ¼ tsp. English mustard powder • ½ lb. cheddar, shredded • 1 tbsp. freshly grated Parmesan

SERVES 4

After mixing, the soufflé mixture can be kept in a refrigerator for an hour or two but should be served immediately after baking as the dramatic rise won't last for ever. This cheese soufflé has a crisp Parmesan crust and a delicious soft center.

1. Preheat the oven to 350° F. Grease a 5½ cup soufflé dish with butter. Melt the butter in a large saucepan, add the flour, and cook for 1 minute. Whisk in the milk, then bring to a boil, stirring until thickened. Remove from the heat and add the nutmeg, mustard, and seasoning. Stir in the cheese and let cool a few minutes.

2. Whisk in the egg yolks. Whisk the egg whites until stiff but not dry, beat in 1 tbsp., then fold in the rest.

3. Pour the mixture into the soufflé dish and run your finger around the top inside edge. Sprinkle with Parmesan and bake, 30–40 minutes.

Apple and Calvados soufflé

3 tbsp. butter, plus extra for greasing • 1 tbsp. graham cracker crumbs • 3 tbsp. all-purpose flour • ¾ cup milk • 3 tbsp. Calvados or other apple brandy • 2 tart apples, peeled, cored, and sliced • 2 tsp. grated lemon peel • 2 tbsp. fresh lemon juice • ½ cup sugar • 4 eggs, separated • confectioners' sugar for dusting

SERVES 4

A delicious dessert, this fantastic soufflé combines tart apples with sweet Calvados. Individual dishes look the most impressive but if you don't have them one large one will do.

1. Grease six 1¼ cup soufflé dishes or a 7½ cup soufflé dish with butter and scatter the graham cracker crumbs around the sides and over the base. Preheat the oven to 375° F.

2. Melt the remaining butter in a saucepan and add the flour. Remove from the heat and gradually stir in the milk. Return the pan to the heat and bring to a boil, whisking gently until it thickens.

3. Cook for 1 minute, then remove from the heat and whisk in the calvados. Cover the sauce with plastic wrap. Set aside to cool.

4. Cook the apples with the lemon peel and juice and 1 tbsp. sugar in a covered pan stirring occasionally until they form a purée, 5–6 minutes. Let cool slightly. Meanwhile whisk the egg yolks into the sauce, then stir in the apple purée.

5. Whisk the egg whites until stiff. Gradually whisk in remaining sugar until the meringue is glossy. Stir a spoonful of the whites into the sauce then fold in the rest. Spoon dishes, run a finger around the edge and bake, 20–35 minutes, depending on dish size. Dust the top with confectioners' sugar before serving.

Mushroom and garlic soufflé

For the sauce • **1½ tbsp. butter, plus extra for greasing** • **1½ tbsp. all-purpose flour** • **1 cup milk** • **pinch grated nutmeg** • **2 oz. mild goats' cheese** • **4 eggs, separated**
For the flavoring • **1 tbsp. butter** • **10 oz. chestnut or field mushrooms, halved and finely sliced** • **2 garlic cloves, minced** • **2 tbsp. freshly chopped parsley** • **1 tsp. fresh thyme leaves**

SERVES 4

Use mushrooms with a good strong flavor and a low water content such as chestnut or field mushrooms as they will give the best result. This recipe would be ideal to serve as a starter served with a mixed green salad.

1. Preheat the oven to 375° F. Grease a 6¼ cup soufflé dish with butter. Melt the butter in a large saucepan, add the flour and cook, 1 minute. Whisk in the milk then bring to a boil whisking until the sauce has thickened. Remove from the heat and add the nutmeg and seasoning. Stir in the cheese and let cool a few minutes.

2. For the flavoring, melt the butter in a large skillet and cook the mushrooms over a medium heat until softened and all the liquid has evaporated. Stir in the garlic, cook for 1 minute then let cool.

3. Whisk the egg yolks into the sauce, one at a time until well incorporated and the sauce is smooth and glossy. Stir in the mushrooms and herbs.

4. With a clean whisk, whisk the egg whites until stiff. Stir a large spoonful of the egg whites into the sauce to slacken it a bit, then gently fold in the rest.

5. Pour the mixture into the soufflé dish. Run your finger around the edge and bake, 30–35 minutes.

Sweet vanilla soufflé

1 cup milk • 1 vanilla bean, split • 1/2 cup sugar • 4 tbsp. butter • 4 tbsp. all-purpose flour • 3 large eggs, separated • 1 egg white • confectioners' sugar, for dusting

SERVES 6

This light and airy dessert makes a delicious end to any special meal.

1. Bring the milk, vanilla bean, and sugar to a boil very slowly, then set aside to cool.

2. Scrape the vanilla seeds out of the beans with the point of a sharp knife and add to the milk. Discard the bean. Melt the butter in a small saucepan and stir in the flour. Cook 1 minute. Remove from the heat and gradually stir in the milk. Return the pan to the heat and bring to a boil, stirring all the time.

3. Cook for 1 minute, then remove from the heat and cover the surface of the sauce with plastic wrap. Set aside to cool slightly.

4. Preheat the oven to 375° F. Liberally butter six ¾ cup soufflé dishes and dust the insides with sugar. Whisk the egg yolks into the cooled sauce until smooth. Whisk the egg whites until stiff. Spoon half into the sauce and fold in gently with a metal spoon. Fold in the remaining egg whites.

5. Pour into the dishes. Bake until well risen and lightly set, 20–25 minutes. Dust the tops with confectioners' sugar before serving.

Spinach roulade

6 oz. fresh spinach • 3 tbsp. all-purpose flour, plus extra for dusting • 3 tbsp. butter, plus extra for greasing • scant 2 cups milk • ¼ tsp. grated nutmeg • 3 medium eggs, separated • 4 tbsp. freshly grated Parmesan cheese • 1 package garlic and herb cream cheese • ⅓ cup ricotta • 2 tbsp. sour cream • 2 tbsp. fresh snipped chives

SERVES 6 as a starter or 4 as a main course

Another delicious presentation of a soufflé, this time as as a soft, puffy roulade.

1. Preheat the oven to 400° F. Wash the spinach and cook in a covered saucepan until just wilted, 2–3 minutes. Cool slightly, squeeze out all the moisture and finely chop. Grease and line a 9 x 13-inch jelly roll pan with waxed paper. Grease the paper and dust lightly with flour.

2. Melt the butter in a saucepan and stir in the flour. Cook for 1 minute, then remove from the heat. Gradually whisk in the milk, then return to the heat and continue whisking until the mixture boils and thickens. Boil for 1 minute, then remove from the heat.

3. Whisk in the egg yolks one at a time until the mixture is smooth. Beat in the spinach, seasoning, and nutmeg.

4. Whisk the egg whites until stiff and fold into the mixture. Pour the mixture into the pan and spread over evenly. Bake until lightly set, 12–14 minutes.

5. Sprinkle the Parmesan over a sheet of waxed paper and turn the roulade out onto it. Remove the lining paper and allow to cool slightly. Beat the garlic and herb cheese, ricotta, sour cream, and chives together. Spread the mix over the roulade, then use the paper to roll it up from one long side. Serve sliced with a mixed green salad.

Festive chocolate and hazelnut roulade

6 oz. unsweetened chocolate • 6 eggs, separated • ⅔ cup sugar • ½ cup ground
hazelnuts • confectioners' sugar, for dredging
For the whipped cream • 1 cup cream • 1 tbsp. brandy

SERVES 6–8

**This special dessert is really easy to make—start in the
morning, before the meal or even the day before. If
serving at Christmas decorate with chocolate holly leaves
before dusting with extra confectioners' sugar.**

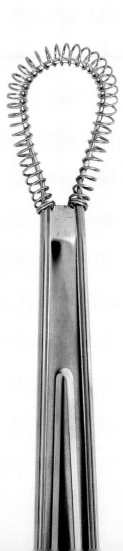

1. Preheat the oven to 350° F. Grease and line a 9 x 13-inch jelly
roll pan with waxed paper. Melt the chocolate in a bowl set over hot
water, then set aside to cool slightly.

2. Whisk the egg yolks and sugar until the mixture is thick, smooth,
and glossy. In a separate bowl with a clean whisk, whisk the egg
whites until stiff.

3. Fold the cooled chocolate and the ground hazelnuts into the egg
yolk mixture. Gently stir in half the egg whites, then fold in the rest.
Pour the mixture into the prepared pan, then bake until risen and
firm to the touch, 20 minutes. Cool in the pan, covered with a
cooling rack and clean damp dishtowel.

4. Whip the cream and brandy together until it forms soft peaks.
Liberally dredge a piece of waxed paper with confectioners' sugar,
then turn the roulade out onto it. Peel off the lining paper and
spread over the cream.

5. Use the paper to help you roll the roulade from one long side.
Transfer to a plate while still wrapped in the rolling paper. Remove
the paper and sift extra sugar over it if needed. Cut into slices and
serve with extra whipped cream if desired.

Cherry and berry roulade

5 large eggs, separated • generous ½ cup sugar • 3 oz. creamed coconut, grated • confectioners' sugar, for dredging • 2 tbsp. flaked coconut
For the whipped cream • ½ lb. mixed frozen summer fruits with cherries • 1 tbsp. fresh orange juice • 2 tsp. cornstarch • 2 tsp. kirsch • ½ cup whipping cream

SERVES 6–8

The featherlight sponge cake encloses a sumptuous selection of berries and a kirsch-flavored whipped cream.

1. Preheat the oven to 350° F. Grease and line a 9 x 13-inch jelly roll pan with waxed paper. Whisk the egg yolks and sugar until the mixture is thick smooth and glossy. In a separate bowl, whisk the egg whites until stiff.

2. Fold the coconut into the egg yolk mixture. Gently stir in half the egg whites, then fold in the rest. Pour the mixture into the prepared pan, then bake until risen and firm to the touch, 20 minutes. Cool in the pan covered with a cooling rack and a clean damp dishtowel.

3. Cook the fruit in a saucepan with the orange juice, until the juices begin to run. Blend the cornstarch with a little water and stir into the fruit. Cook until thickened, then remove from the heat and set aside to cool. Whip the cream and kirsch together until it forms soft peaks. Liberally dredge a piece of waxed paper with confectioners' sugar, then turn the roulade out onto it. Peel off the lining paper and spread on the whipped cream and then the fruit.

4. Use the paper underneath to help you roll the roulade from one of the long sides so that it doesn't crack. Transfer to a plate while still wrapped in the rolling paper. Top with flaked coconut and sift extra confectioners' sugar on top if needed. Cut into slices and serve with extra whipped cream as desired.

Apricot and almond soufflé omelet

2 eggs, separated • 2 tbsp. sugar, plus extra to serve • butter, for frying • 2 tbsp. apricot jelly, to serve • 1 tbsp. fresh orange juice • 4 canned apricot halves, sliced • 1 tbsp. toasted flaked almonds

SERVES 2

Whisked egg whites folded into the basic mixture make a wonderfully light, puffy soufflé omelet that can be served with all sorts of fillings. The most simple is warmed jelly.

1. Whisk the egg yolks and sugar in a bowl with a hand-held electric mixer until thick. In another bowl, with clean beaters, whisk the whites until they form stiff peaks.

2. Fold the egg whites into the egg yolk mixture until incorporated.

3. Melt the butter in a small ovenproof skillet. Add the omelet mixture, and cook until well risen and golden underneath, 2–3 minutes. Place the skillet under a hot broiler, 1 minute, to finish cooking.

4. Melt the jelly with the orange juice, boil for 1 minute then stir in the sliced apricots. Spoon over the top of the omelet and fold over quickly. Tip onto a plate and scatter with the flaked almonds. Dust with sugar.

Butterscotch, pecan, and banana soufflé omelet

For the sauce • 1 ½ tbsp. butter • 3 tbsp. golden brown sugar • 1 tbsp. corn syrup •
4 tbsp. whipping cream • 2 tbsp. pecan nuts broken into pieces
For the omelet • 2 eggs, separated • 2 tbsp. sugar, plus extra for dusting • 1 tbsp. butter
To serve • vanilla ice cream • 1 banana, sliced

SERVES 1–2

**This light and fluffy sweet omelet is topped with sliced
bananas, vanilla ice cream, and a special pecan and
butterscotch sauce—a great combination of hot and cold.**

1. First make the sauce. Melt the butter, sugar, and syrup together
in a small saucepan. Stir in the cream and nuts and bring to a boil.
Remove from the heat and set aside.

2. For the omelet, put the egg yolks in a bowl with the sugar and
whisk until the mixture is thick and creamy.

3. In another bowl, with clean beaters, whisk the egg whites until
stiff. Fold into the egg yolk mixture until evenly incorporated.

4. Melt the butter in a small skillet and add the omelet mixture
spreading over the base with a palette knife. Cook until well risen
and golden underneath, 2–3 minutes. Place the skillet under a hot
broiler until pale golden on top, 1 minute.

5. Slide the omelet onto a plate and top one side with ice cream
and bananas. Drizzle with the sauce and flip the other side of the
omelet to enclose the filling. Dust with sugar and serve at once.

Goat cheese and arugula omelet

For the omelet • **3 eggs** • **¼ tsp. fresh thyme leaves** • **2 tbsp. grated Parmesan cheese** • **1 tbsp. butter**
For the filling • **6 cherry tomatoes, sliced** • **6 pitted black olives, sliced** • **3 oz. mild soft goat cheese** • **handful of arugula or baby spinach leaves, washed** • **1 tsp. vinaigrette dressing**

SERVES 1–2

This savory version of a soufflé omelet makes a really simple, light but delicious supper. With a topping of goat cheese, tomatoes, arugula, and olives, it has a real Mediterranean flavor to it.

1. Break 2 eggs into a bowl, separate the remaining egg and add the yolk to the eggs. Using a hand-held electric mixer, whisk the eggs until thick and foamy. Clean the beaters and whisk the egg white in a separate bowl until stiff.

2. Fold the egg white into the eggs with the thyme leaves, Parmesan, and some seasoning. Melt the butter in a small skillet and pour in the egg mixture. Cook over a medium heat until golden underneath, 1–2 minutes.

3. Put the pan under a hot broiler and broil until golden, 1 minute. Top one half with the tomato and olives then dot over spoonfuls of the goat cheese. Toss the arugula in the dressing and add to the omelet. Flip over the uncovered half of the omelet and slide onto a plate.

batters

batters

batters A batter at its simplest is a mixture based on flour and eggs that has a pouring consistency. Different batters serve different purposes: crepes, pancakes, griddle cakes, and waffles are delicious served on their own or with sweet or savory fillings or toppings, and variations on the batter mix can make a wealth of desserts or savory snacks. Another use of batter is for coating foods before frying; fish or vegetables particularly benefit from this.

crepes the basic method Crepes are thin, frilly pancakes, made with a richer batter containing more eggs. If you want a fatter, fluffier pancake, follow the Griddle Cakes steps on page 116.

step 1 Sift the flour into a bowl with the salt and make a well in the center. Break the eggs into the well and add a little of the milk. Gradually draw the flour in, then whisk well until smooth.

step 2 Add the remaining milk and whisk in gently until the batter is smooth with the consistency of light cream. Make sure you don't overwhip the batter at this stage.

step 3 Heat a heavy-based or nonstick skillet or crepe pan and add a little of the clarified butter. Add a small ladleful of the batter and swirl around the base of the skillet until evenly coated. Cook until golden, 1–2 minutes, then flip over and cook on the other side, another 1–2 minutes. Transfer to a plate. Repeat with the remaining mixture, adding a little more clarified butter between crepes until all the mixture is used up. The crepes can be reheated in the oven before serving.

Crepes suzette

⅔ cup all-purpose flour • pinch salt • 2 large eggs • 1¼ cups milk • clarified butter, for frying
For the orange butter • 1 stick butter • 2 tbsp. confectioners' sugar • 1 tbsp. grated orange peel
To finish • 2 tbsp. fresh orange juice • 3 tbsp. brandy • 4 tbsp. orange liqueur

SERVES 4

The classic French crepe recipe, this makes an impressive dinner party dessert, especially when you flambé the crepes in front of the guests.

1. Prepare your crepes following the steps above.

2. For the orange butter, soften the butter with a small whisk, then whisk in the confectioners' sugar and orange peel. Spread a little butter onto each crepe, then return each in turn to a large skillet, butter side down. Cook over a low heat until the butter has melted and the crepe is warmed through. Fold into quarters and slide to the side of the pan.

4. When all have been returned to the pan, pour over the orange juice and heat through.

5. Immediately before serving, pour on the brandy and orange liqueur. Light the sauce carefully with a lighter, making sure to keep all hair and clothing away from the flame. Allow the flames to die down then serve with vanilla ice cream.

Summer berry crepes

For the crepes • scant 1 cup all-purpose flour • pinch salt • 1 large egg • 1 cup milk • a few drops vanilla extract • 1 tbsp. butter • 1 tbsp. sunflower oil
For the fruit • 1 tbsp. butter • 4 tbsp. sugar • 1 tsp. grated orange peel • 5 tbsp. fresh orange juice • ¾ lb. mixed summer fruits, e.g. strawberries, raspberries, blueberries • 2 tbsp. white rum • 1 tbsp. confectioners' sugar • whipped cream to serve • fresh fruit or mint leaves, to decorate (optional)

SERVES 4

Crepes make a wonderful dessert when teamed with seasonal fruits. These can be made ahead of time and reheated in the fruit and syrup in the pan.

1. Sift the flour into a bowl with the salt and make a well in the center. Break in the egg and gradually add half the milk, whisking briskly to draw the flour into the egg.

2. Whisk in the remaining milk, vanilla extract, and 4 tbsp. water to make a smooth batter which has the consistency of light cream.

3. Heat a small, nonstick skillet and add the butter and oil. When the butter has melted, pour into a small bowl and return the pan to the heat. Add a small ladleful of the batter mixture and swirl around the base of the pan until evenly coated. Cook until golden then flip over and cook on the other side, 1–2 minutes total. Remove from the pan and slide onto a plate. Repeat with the remaining mixture, adding a little butter and oil between crepes.

4. For the fruit, melt the butter in a saucepan, stir in the sugar, and cook gently for 1–2 minutes. Add the orange peel and juice and swirl the pan until the sugar has dissolved. Add the fruit and rum and cook until the fruit juices begin to run. Fold two crepes onto each serving plate and top with a spoonful of the fruit. Serve with cream and decorate with fresh fruit or mint.

Rich chocolate tarts

¾ lb. sweet shortcrust pastry • 4 oz. unsweetened chocolate • 2 eggs • 1 ½ tbsp. sugar • ½ cup whipping cream

SERVES 6

These little tarts are filled with a wonderful chocolate batter that puffs up and just wobbles when it is cooked. Serve as a special treat with custard or cream.

1. Preheat the oven to 400° F. Divide the pastry into six pieces. Roll out each piece thinly and use to line six individual tartlet pans. Chill for 20 minutes. Prick the bases and line with waxed paper and baking beans. Bake blind, 15 minutes.

2. Remove the paper and beans and return to the oven, an additional 5 minutes. Remove from the oven and set aside. Reduce the oven temperature to 375° F.

3. Melt the chocolate in a bowl set over a pan of simmering water. Allow to cool slightly. Whisk the eggs and sugar in a bowl until pale. Whisk in the cream, then the melted chocolate. Pour the chocolate batter into the tartlet cases and bake until set, 15 minutes.

Cherry and almond clafoutis

2 tbsp. butter • 1 lb. black cherries • 2 tbsp. all-purpose flour • ⅓ cup confectioners'
sugar • 4 eggs • 1 cup creamy milk • 2 tbsp. kirsch • 2 tbsp. flaked almonds

SERVES 4

1. Preheat the oven to 350° F. Use the butter to grease a 5-cup
dish. Scatter the cherries over the base.

2. Sift the flour and confectioners' sugar together into a bowl and
gradually whisk in the eggs until the mixture is smooth. Whisk in the
milk and then stir in the kirsch.

3. Pour the batter over the cherries, then scatter over the flaked
almonds. Bake until lightly set, 35–40 minutes. Cool slightly then
dust with confectioners' sugar before serving.

**This is a classic recipe
for clafoutis, a type of
batter pudding from the
Limousin region of France
where they grow cherries
in abundance.**

Burnt custard laced with bourbon

1 ¾ cups whipping cream • 1 vanilla bean, split • 5 egg yolks • ½ cup sugar • 4 tbsp.
bourbon

SERVES 4

1. Preheat the oven to 400° F. Heat the cream and vanilla bean
over a low heat until almost boiling, then leave to infuse for 10
minutes. Whisk the egg yolks with 5 tbsp. of the sugar in a bowl
until pale and thickened slightly. Stir in the hot cream and bourbon.

2. Pour into four 4-ounce ramekins and put them in a roasting
pan. Pour in warm water to come half way up the sides. Bake until
a skin has formed, but the custard is still wobbly, 12–15 minutes.

3. Chill the ramekins for at least 3 hours. Scatter the remaining
sugar over the tops. Cook under a hot broiler or use a small blow
torch to caramelize the sugar. Allow the caramel to cool and harden
before serving.

**This boozy version of a
crème brûlée is truly out
of this world. The custard
should be lightly set in
the middle with a thin
crisp golden caramel on
top.**

Luxury black currant pudding

8 medium thick slices of bread, crusts removed · ½ stick butter at room temperature ·
½ lb. fresh or frozen black currants · 5 eggs · ⅓ cup sugar · 2½ cups creamy milk (or
even better, half-and-half) · 2 tsp. vanilla extract · freshly grated nutmeg · 1 tbsp.
coarse sugar

SERVES 4

**Fresh black currants add a refreshing tang to this
luxurious bread and butter pudding. Let the pudding
stand for a while before eating or even better, serve cold
with extra cream.**

1. Preheat the oven to 350° F. Spread the bread with the butter
then cut diagonally in half. Generously butter a 2½-quart baking
dish. Layer the bread slices in the dish, buttered side up, scattering
the black currants between the layers as you go.

2. Whisk the eggs and sugar together lightly in a mixing bowl then
gradually whisk in the milk or milk and cream, the vanilla extract,
and a large pinch of grated nutmeg.

3. Pour the batter over the bread, pushing the slices down well to
soak them thoroughly, scatter with the sugar and some more grated
nutmeg. Place the dish in a baking pan a quarter filled with hot
water. Bake until the top is crisp and golden, 1 hour.

4. Let cool slightly then serve with lightly whipped cream.

Griddle cakes

⅔ cup all-purpose flour • 1 tsp. baking soda • ¾ tsp. baking powder • 1 egg • 4 tbsp. melted butter • 1¼ cups buttermilk • scant ½ cup milk

To serve • 12 slices bacon • 2 oz. baby spinach leaves • generous ½ cup sour cream • ground black pepper, to garnish

SERVES 4

The batter for griddle pancakes has a thicker consistency and is lightened with a rising agent. Sweeten and serve as a dessert or if no sugar is added, as a savory.

1. Sift the flour, baking soda, and baking powder into a bowl. Add the egg.

2. Add the butter, buttermilk, and milk and use a balloon whisk to whisk everything together until the mixture is smooth.

3. Heat a heavy-based skillet or griddle. Wipe over a little oil then drop spoonfuls into the skillet. Cook until bubbles appear on the surface and they are golden brown underneath. Quickly flip them over and cook until golden. Remove from the skillet and keep warm.

4. Broil the bacon slices until crispy. Top a pile of griddle cakes with spinach leaves, the crisp cooked bacon, and a spoonful of sour cream. Garnish with black pepper.

Pancakes with tropical fruit and maple syrup

⅔ cup all-purpose flour • 1 tsp. baking soda • ¾ tsp. baking powder • 1 tbsp. sugar • 1 tsp. vanilla extract • 1 egg, beaten • 4 tbsp. melted butter • 1¼ cups buttermilk • oil for frying • 1 lb. prepared mixed island fruits, e.g., pineapple, mango, papaya, kiwi, cut into bite sized pieces • 1 cup Greek or plain yogurt • maple syrup to drizzle

MAKES 12 pancakes

These fluffy pancakes make an ideal brunch served topped with fresh fruit, a spoonful of tangy yogurt, and a good drizzle of maple syrup. Alternatively, serve spread with a little butter and a spoonful of fruit preserves for afternoon snack.

1. Sift the flour, baking soda, baking powder, and sugar into a bowl. Add the vanilla extract, the egg, butter, and buttermilk and whisk until the mixture is smooth.

2. Heat a heavy-based skillet or griddle. Wipe over a little oil, then drop spoonfuls into the skillet. Cook until bubbles appear on the surface and the pancakes are golden brown underneath. Flip them over and cook until golden. Remove from the skillet and keep warm. Repeat with the remaining batter.

3. Combine the fruit in a bowl. Place three pancakes on each plate and spoon some yogurt on top. Add some of the fruit and drizzle with maple syrup before serving.

Peach, pecan, and caramel waffles

For the waffles • 1 ½ cups all-purpose flour • 2 tsp. baking powder • 1 tsp. baking soda • 2 eggs • 4 tbsp. melted butter • ¾ cup milk • 1¼ cups buttermilk • 1 tsp. vanilla extract
To serve • 2 peaches • ½ cup pecan nuts, chopped • 1 tbsp. brown sugar • 5 tbsp. maple syrup • 3 tbsp. dark rum

MAKES 8–10 waffles

Waffles use a similar batter to the griddle cakes, but they have a little more rising agent and liquid—buttermilk or milk or a combination of the two.

1. First make the waffles. Sift the dry ingredients into a large bowl. Then whisk in the eggs, butter, and milk, gradually incorporating the flour until smooth.

2. Add the buttermilk and vanilla extract to the mixture. Cover and let stand, 30 minutes. Heat an electric waffle iron and pour a ladleful over two-thirds of the iron. Close it and wipe off any excess batter.

3. Cook for 3–4 minutes, following the manufacturer's instructions.

4. When the batter stops steaming open the iron and lift out the waffle with a fork. Keep hot in the oven.

5. Slice the peaches into wedges and spread over a baking tray. Scatter the pecans over the top and then sprinkle over the brown sugar. Drizzle with the maple syrup and dark rum and cook under a hot broiler until the sugar is bubbling and the pecans are golden.

6. Spoon the peaches and pecans on top of the waffles and drizzle over some of the juices.

Corn cakes with shrimp salsa

For the cakes • scant 1 cup all-purpose flour • 1 tsp. baking soda • ¾ tsp. baking powder •
1 large egg • 4 tbsp. melted butter • 1¼ cups buttermilk • 2 cups canned corn, drained
For the salsa • ½ lb. peeled shrimp • ½ cucumber, peeled and diced • 6 tomatoes, diced •
1 red onion, quartered and finely sliced • 1 avocado, diced • 1 tbsp. lime juice • 2 tbsp.
olive oil • a handful of fresh chopped cilantro • 1 red chili, finely chopped

MAKES 12 cakes

**Corn cakes accompany all types of food really well.
Topped with this refreshing shrimp salsa they make a
wonderful lunch or supper.**

1. Sift the flour, baking soda, and baking powder into a bowl. Add
the egg, butter, and buttermilk and whisk until smooth. Stir in the
corn and set aside.

2. Heat a heavy-based skillet or griddle. Wipe over a little oil, then
drop spoonfuls of the mixture into the skillet. Spread out lightly to
rough rounds then cook over a low heat until bubbles appear on the
surface and they are dark golden brown underneath. Flip them over
and cook until golden and firm to the touch. Remove from the pan
and repeat with the remaining mixture.

3. Meanwhile make the salsa by combining everything in a bowl
and mixing together well. Serve with the corn cakes.

Cheddar muffins

scant 2 cups cornmeal • scant 1 ¼ cups all-purpose flour • 1 ½ tbsp. baking powder • ½ tsp. salt • 4 oz. cheddar cheese, shredded • 1 small onion, shredded • ¼ tsp. chopped red chili • 1 tbsp. snipped fresh chives • 3 large eggs • 1 ¾ cups milk • 1 stick melted butter

MAKES 12

Traditional American muffins are made with a thick batter but it shouldn't be overmixed or the muffins will be tough. All the mixing is done when you whisk the eggs and milk together. When the flour is gently folded in, the mixture will be very lumpy, but that is how it is supposed to be. These cheese and onion flavored muffins make great savory snacks to put in a packed lunch or can be served with soups, stews, and casseroles. The mixture can be baked as a whole in a greased cake pan.

1. Preheat the oven to 400° F. Line a 12-muffin pan with muffin papers and set aside. Sift the cornmeal, flour, baking powder, and salt together in a bowl. Stir in the cheese, onion, chili, and chives. Use a balloon whisk to whisk the eggs, milk, and butter together well.

2. Stir the eggs, milk, and butter into the flour mixture until combined but do not beat. It should still be quite lumpy.

3. Spoon the mixture into the muffin cases and bake until well risen, lightly golden, and firm to the touch, 20 minutes. Serve warm.

Red snapper in crisp beer batter

⅔ cup all-purpose flour • pinch salt • 2 eggs, separated • 1 tbsp. peanut oil • ¾ cup beer or ale • four 5 oz. red snapper or trout fillets, halved • peanut oil for deep frying • lemon slices, to serve

SERVES 4

The consistency of this batter can be varied by adding more or less liquid, in this case, beer. A runny consistency will produce a light thin batter, and a thick one will cling better but be a bit more mushy. Adding beaten egg whites makes it a bit lighter. Serve with fried potatoes and a green salad.

1. Sift the flour into a bowl and add the salt. Make a well in the center and whisk in the egg yolks, oil, and the beer. Whisk until combined but still lumpy.

2. Leave to rest for 30 minutes. Beat the egg whites in a nonreactive bowl until stiff and fold into the batter.

3. Heat the peanut oil for deep frying to 375° F. Quickly dip two fish fillets into the batter, allowing excess to drain back into the bowl. Gently lower into the oil and fry, turning often until the batter is golden, 2–3 minutes. Drain on paper towels and keep hot while frying the remaining fish. Serve with lemon slices.

Shrimp and vegetable tempura

1 egg • 1 cup ice cold water • ½ cup all-purpose flour, sifted • ⅓ cup cornstarch • peanut oil for deep frying • ½ lb. raw tiger shrimp, peeled and deveined • 1 zucchini, thickly sliced • ½ small eggplant, cut into strips • 4-oz. can baby corn, halved lengthwise • 1 large red bell pepper, deseeded and cut into thick strips • 2 small red onions, cut into wedges
To serve • 4 tbsp. Japanese soy sauce • 1 scallion, finely chopped • 1 red chili, finely chopped

SERVES 4

Tempura batter is very light as it uses water rather than milk, and the water must be ice cold. Here it coats a selection of vegetables and raw shrimp but it's equally good with scallops and squid. Serve with a wedge of lemon if you prefer it to the Japanese-style dip.

1. Whisk the egg and ice cold water together in a bowl. Sift the flours together then add to the egg mixture and whisk very briefly to combine. The lumps will keep the batter light when it's fried.

2. Heat the oil for deep-frying to 375° F. Dip a few shrimp and pieces of the vegetables into the batter and add to the hot oil. Fry until lightly golden, 2–3 minutes. Remove with a slotted spoon and drain on paper towels. Fry the rest of the shrimp and vegetables in the same way.

3. Mix the soy sauce with the scallion and chili and serve in a bowl with the shrimp and vegetables.

sauces

sauces

Many classic sauces are made using whisking techniques. Emulsified sauces like mayonnaise are made by whisking oil, egg yolks, and vinegar, and in the case of aioli, by injecting garlic. Hollandaise and béarnaise sauces call for the same technique, but use butter instead of oil and are served hot. Use tasty butter sauces to enrich main courses by whisking butter into a reduction of wine, or create mouthwatering sweet sauces to top off desserts.

mayonnaise-style sauces the basic method

Mayonnaise and other emulsified sauces work best if the ingredients are at room temperature before you start. The usual ratio is ¾ cup oil per egg yolk.

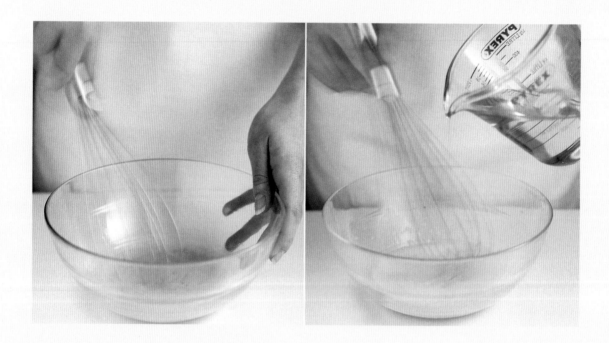

step 1 Using a balloon or egg whisk, whisk the egg yolk, seasoning, vinegar, and mustard together until they thicken slightly. This should take about 1 minute.

step 2 Measure the oil in a measuring cup. Add the oil a drop at a time, whisking constantly. Keep whisking until it begins to thicken and lighten, after 2 tbsp. oil have been added.

step 3 Now you can start adding the oil more quickly. Holding the cup steady and whisking all the time, add the oil in a thin steady stream, but not all at once.

step 4 When all the oil has been added and whisked into the mayonnaise, taste it, adding more salt and pepper if necessary, then stir in any flavoring ingredients.

Lemon herb mayonnaise with swordfish kebabs

For the mayonnaise • 1 egg yolk • 1 tbsp. white wine vinegar • ½ tsp. Dijon mustard • ¾ cup peanut or light olive oil
For the flavoring • 2 tsp. grated lemon peel • 1 tbsp. chopped fresh tarragon • 1 tbsp. chopped capers • 1 tbsp. chopped fresh parsley
For the kebabs • 1 lb. swordfish steaks, cut into bite size pieces • 2 red onions, cut into 6 wedges • 2 limes, each cut into wedges • 2 tbsp. olive oil • 1 lime, pared zest • 1 tsp. fresh thyme leaves • 2 tbsp. maple syrup   **SERVES 4**

All sorts of flavorings can be added to the basic mayonnaise. This lemon herb version goes really well with the swordfish kebabs.

1. For the mayonnaise, whisk the egg yolk, seasoning, vinegar, and mustard together until they thicken slightly.

2. Add the oil a drop at a time whisking continuously. When the sauce begins to thicken and lighten start adding the oil in a thin steady stream, whisking continuously.

3. When all the oil has been added, taste for seasoning, then stir in the lemon, tarragon, capers, and parsley. Set aside.

4. Put the swordfish, red onion, and lime wedges into a bowl and toss in the oil, lime peel, thyme leaves, and maple syrup. Chill 2–3 hours. Thread the fish, lime wedges, and red onion onto eight skewers and cook under a hot broiler 5–6 minutes turning often until starting to color on the outside. Serve the kebabs with a spoonful of the sauce, new potatoes, and a side salad.

Tomato and olive salad with basil mayonnaise

For the mayonnaise • 1 egg yolk • 2 tsp. balsamic vinegar • 1 tsp. Dijon mustard • ⅔ cup peanut oil • 2 tsp. pesto sauce • pinch of sugar

For the salad • 2 beefsteak or Delizia tomatoes, sliced thickly • 6 oz. yellow cherry tomatoes, halved • 6 oz. baby plum tomatoes, halved • 4-inch piece cucumber, peeled and sliced • 1 red onion, thinly sliced • handful arugula leaves • 4 oz. feta cheese, crumbled • ½ cup mixed marinated olives

SERVES 4

These three ingredients work really well together and together with tangy feta cheese make a perfect salad for a summer lunch. Make sure the tomatoes are at room temperature to bring out the best flavor.

1. For the basil mayonnaise, whisk the egg yolks, seasoning, 1 tsp. vinegar, and mustard together until they thicken slightly. This should take about 1 minute.

2. Add the oil a drop at a time whisking constantly. When the sauce begins to thicken and lighten—after about 1 tbsp. of the oil has been added—start adding the oil in a thin steady stream whisking continuously.

3. When all the oil has been added, stir in the remaining vinegar. Season then add the pesto and sugar and set aside.

4. Combine all the tomatoes on a large platter. Scatter over the cucumber, onion, arugula, feta, and olives. Serve with a spoonful of the basil mayonnaise and warm bread.

Salmon and dill cakes with hollandaise sauce

For the salmon cakes • **7 oz. raw tiger shrimp, peeled** • **1 lb. skinned salmon fillet, finely chopped** • **1 tbsp. drained capers, chopped** • **2 tbsp. fresh chopped dill** • **2 scallions, finely chopped** • **2 tsp. grated lemon peel** • **½ cup fresh white bread crumbs** • For the hollandaise • **¾ cup butter** • **3 egg yolks** • **1 tbsp. fresh lemon juice**

SERVES 4

The key to a good hollandaise sauce is gentle heat and plenty of whisking. The resulting sauce should be a stable creamy emulsion of egg yolks and butter, flavored with either a reduction of vinegar, wine, or more commonly lemon juice. Serve while still warm.

1. First make the salmon cakes. Blend the tiger shrimp in a food processor to a paste. Put into a bowl with the salmon fillet, capers, dill, scallions, lemon peel, seasoning, and bread crumbs. Shape into small cakes and chill for at least 1 hour before using.

2. Melt the butter in a saucepan over a low heat. Remove from the heat and let cool slightly. Put 2 tbsp. water and the egg yolks in a bowl and set over a saucepan of gently simmering water. Season and whisk until the yolks form a pale thick mousse that leaves a ribbon trail on the surface for 5 seconds.

3. Gradually pour in the melted butter, whisking continuously. Discard any sediment left in the bottom of the butter pan.

4. Whisk in the lemon juice and season to taste. If the consistency is too thick, add a little boiling water, a spoonful at a time, until the required consistency is reached.

5. Cook the salmon cakes on a hot oiled griddle, 8–10 minutes. Serve with an avocado and tomato salad with a spoonful of the hollandaise sauce on the side.

Grilled shrimp with aioli

For the aioli • 1 egg yolk • 2 garlic cloves • ½ tsp. Dijon mustard • 1 tbsp. fresh lemon juice • pinch sugar • generous ½ cup light olive oil

To serve • 12 fresh asparagus spears, about 9 oz. • 12 large uncooked shrimp • oil for brushing • pinch of ground paprika, to garnish • freshly chopped parsley, to garnish

SERVES 4

Aioli is a wonderful garlic mayonnaise favored in the South of France that goes well with all types of foods, but especially well with fish and asparagus. Serve with grilled vegetables or serve with burgers instead of regular mayonnaise.

1. Place the egg yolk, garlic, mustard, lemon juice, sugar, and seasoning in a bowl and whisk together briefly using a spiral whisk.

2. Gradually whisk in the oil, pouring in a thin stream, until thick, then chill until required.

3. Blanch the asparagus spears in boiling salted water, 3 minutes. Drain and put in a bowl of cold water to stop the spears from overcooking.

4. Heat a large griddle pan or barbecue, brush the shrimp with oil and cook, 2–3 minutes each side. Set aside. Cook the asparagus spears in the same way, until lightly charred, 1–2 minutes. Garnish with paprika and parsley and serve with the aioli.

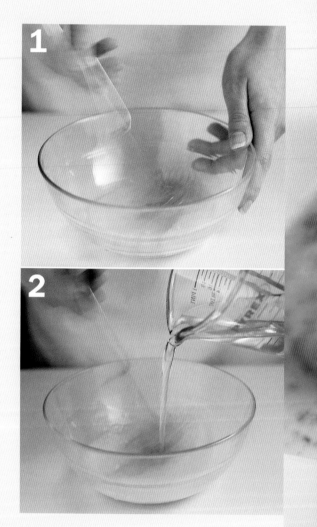

Thyme and orange chicken with herb beurre blanc

For the butter sauce • 1 tbsp. white wine • 2 tbsp. white wine vinegar • 1 shallot, finely chopped • 1 tbsp. whipping cream • ½ cup very cold butter, cubed

For the flavoring • 1 tsp. snipped chives • 2 tsp. torn basil leaves

For the chicken • 4 skinned boned chicken breasts • 2 tbsp. olive oil • 1 tsp fresh thyme leaves • 2 garlic cloves, minced • 2 tsp. grated orange peel • 1 tbsp. fresh orange juice • 1 tbsp. honey

SERVES 4

Butter sauces are made by vigorously whisking small pieces of very cold butter into a wine and vinegar reduction over gentle heat until a smooth emulsion is formed. The aim is to melt the butter into a creamy emulsion rather than becoming an oil that floats on the surface of the sauce. Often served with grilled fish or white meat.

1. Make the herb butter sauce. Boil the wine, vinegar, and shallots in a small heavy-based pan until most of the liquid has evaporated.

2. Add the cream and reduce a little. Whisk the butter a cube at a time into the mixture in the saucepan. Each cube of butter must be emulsified into the sauce before adding the next. Do not allow the sauce to boil. Season to taste and stir in the chives and basil.

3. Put the chicken breasts into a shallow dish and score them with a sharp knife. Add the oil, thyme leaves, garlic, orange peel and juice, honey, and seasoning. Mix together well. Broil the chicken on a rack under a hot broiler, turning once until lightly golden, 8–10 minutes. Serve the chicken with fresh green vegetables, boiled new potatoes, and a spoonful of the butter sauce.

1

2

3

Egg florentine with beurre rouge

For the sauce • generous ⅓ cup red wine • 2 shallots, finely chopped • 1 tbsp. sour cream • 1 cup very cold butter • 1 tsp. sun-dried tomato paste
To serve • 1 tbsp. butter • 1 garlic clove, minced • 1 ½ lbs. baby leaf spinach, washed • 4 large fresh eggs

SERVES 4

This variation of a classic French butter sauce (beurre blan) is made with a reduction of red wine. It is perfect to serve with poached eggs or over vegetables but is also good spooned over peeled grilled shrimp or fish steaks. Serve with toasted ciabatta bread.

1. To make the red butter sauce, boil the wine and shallots in a small heavy-based saucepan until 1 tbsp. of the liquid remains. Add the sour cream and reduce a little. Whisk in the butter, a cube at a time, letting each piece melt into the mixture before adding the next. Season to taste and stir in the tomato paste. Set aside.

2. Heat the butter for the spinach in a saucepan and add garlic. Cook 1 minute then add the spinach, cover and let wilt, 1–2 minutes.

3. Break the eggs into a pan of boiling water and poach until the whites are firm but yolks are still soft, 3–4 minutes. Drain the spinach and spoon onto serving plates. Top with a drained egg and spoon over a little tomato butter sauce. Grind some black pepper over the top before serving.

Provençal beef with béarnaise dressing

For the béarnaise • ¾ cup butter • 3 tbsp. white wine vinegar • 3 tbsp. white wine
10 peppercorns • 3 shallots, finely chopped • 1 tbsp. chopped fresh tarragon • 3 egg yolks •
1 tbsp. fresh chopped mixed chives and parsley
For the beef • 1 ½ lbs. sirloin steak • 7 oz. fine green beans, trimmed and blanched •
3 beefsteak tomatoes , cut into chunky pieces • 14-oz. can lima beans • ½ cup pitted black
olives   **SERVES 4**

A béarnaise sauce is another version of an emulsified sauce with a more pungent flavor. It goes really well with beef or lamb steak.

1. First make the sauce. Melt the butter in a saucepan over a low heat. Remove from the heat and let cool slightly. Pour the vinegar and wine into a pan and add the peppercorns, shallots and tarragon. Bring to a boil and cook until reduced to about 1 tbsp. of liquid. Add 1 tbsp. water to cool the mixture slightly then strain into a bowl.

2. Add the egg yolks to the bowl and set over a saucepan of gently simmering water. Season then whisk until pale and thick or until the whisk leaves a trail on the surface of the mixture for 5 seconds.

3. Gradually pour in the melted butter, whisking continuously, leaving any sediment at the bottom of the butter saucepan. Pour through a sieve and stir in the chives and parsley.

4. Heat a griddle pan. Season the steak and cook to your liking, 5–8 minutes each side. Meanwhile combine the green beans, tomatoes, lima beans, and olives with some seasoning. Remove the steak from the griddle and set aside. Add the vegetables to the hot griddle and cook until heated through, 2 minutes. Divide between four plates. Carve the steak and serve on top of the warm salad with some warm béarnaise sauce drizzled over the top.

Vanilla poached plums with English custard

For the custard • 1 ¼ cups whole milk • ½ vanilla bean, split • 3 egg yolks • 3 tbsp. sugar • ¾ tsp. cornstarch •For the plums • 1 lb. red plums, halved and pitted • 4 tbsp. sugar • ½ vanilla bean, split

SERVES 4

It's helpful to know when making English custard the basic ratio is 1 egg yolk to ⅖ cup whole milk. Adding ¼ tsp. cornstarch per egg yolk will stabilize the custard. After initial whisking, switch to a wooden spoon to stir the custard—you want a creamy consistency rather than a frothy one.

1. Cook the plums. Put the sugar, ¾ cup water, and the vanilla bean in a saucepan. Bring slowly to a boil, stirring until the sugar has dissolved. Boil for 2 minutes, then add the plums, cover, and cook gently until tender, 3–5 minutes. Remove from the heat and set aside.

2. For the custard pour the milk into a saucepan and add the vanilla bean. Bring slowly to a boil, turn off the heat and let infuse, 10 minutes. Remove the vanilla bean.

3. Whisk the egg yolks, sugar, and cornstarch together until thick and lightened. Whisk in the hot milk. Return to a clean heavy-based saucepan and heat gently, stirring all the time until the custard is almost at boiling point and has thickened slightly.

4. Plunge the base of the pan in a bowl of cold water for a few seconds to stop cooking. Spoon the plums into glass bowls and pour some of the custard over the top.

Grilled bananas with chocolate sauce

For the chocolate sauce • 1¼ cups whole milk • ½ vanilla bean, split • 3 egg yolks • 3 tbsp. sugar • ¾ tsp. cornstarch (optional) • 2 oz. unsweetened chocolate, grated
To serve • 4 bananas • 1 tbsp. butter • 3 tbsp. sugar • 4 slices panettone

SERVES 4

This chocolate sauce can be served over any fruit but it goes particularly well with grilled bananas. Try it with poached pears and vanilla ice cream on panettone for an equally delicious variation.

1. For the chocolate sauce pour the milk into a saucepan and add the vanilla bean. Bring slowly to a boil, turn off the heat and let infuse, 10 minutes. Remove the vanilla bean.

2. Whisk the egg yolks, sugar, and cornstarch together until thickened and lightened. Gradually whisk in the hot milk.

3. Return to a clean heavy-based saucepan and heat, gently stirring all the time until the custard is at boiling point and has thickened. Remove from the heat and stir in the chocolate until melted.

4. Heat a griddle pan. Slice the bananas in half lengthwise then in half into four shorter pieces. Dip the long cut side in the butter and then the sugar. Place on the griddle cut-side down and cook until the bananas are lightly browned, 1–2 minutes. Turn over and cook another 30 seconds. Remove from the griddle. Repeat with the panettone, until it is warmed through.

5. Place the panettone on plates and top with the bananas. Drizzle with the chocolate custard to serve.

index